# THE BIG BOOK
## OF
# LUCK & FORTUNE

# THE BIG BOOK
# OF
# LUCK & FORTUNE

## A complete guide to all the most
## Popular Methods of Fortune Telling

*Fully illustrated*

London
W FOULSHAM & CO., LTD.,
NEW YORK   TORONTO   CAPE TOWN   SYDNEY

# CONTENTS

W Foulsham & Co Ltd
Yeovil Road, Slough, Berks, England

ISBN 0-572-01171-7

© W FOULSHAM & CO LTD 1978 & 1982

Printed and bound in Great Britain by
Cox & Wyman Ltd, Reading

# YOUR LUCK

## Your Lucky Day

If all of us were to take careful stock of our lives, it would usually be found that there is one day of the week which stands out before all the other six as our lucky day. With some of us it may be Sunday; with others, Monday; with others, again, Tuesday; and so on until some will agree that all their strokes of good fortune have come to them on Saturdays.

While many of us are plainly conscious of our particular lucky day, there are many more who have never taken sufficient notice of outstanding events to decide which is their own favoured day. Nevertheless, there is one day that outshines all the others and it is on that day that the Fates provide more bounteously for us than they do on any of the other six.

Which is your lucky day? Here is a capital way of finding out. Take a pack of fifty-two cards and, having shuffled them thoroughly, deal off the top ten and discard them.

Then, deal out the next nine cards and place them on the table in a straight line, face down. As soon as this is done, deal out the next eight cards and place them in a line immediately below the first line. Continue by dealing out rows of seven, six, five, four and three cards. In this way, you have seven rows each made up of one card less than there is in the row above it.

Now that the cards are laid out, it is necessary to learn how to read them. The first row stands for Sundays, the second row for Mondays, the third row for Tuesdays, the

fourth row for Wednesdays, the fifth row for Thursdays, the sixth row for Fridays and the seventh row for Saturdays.

With the left hand and not the right, turn over the last card in each row. Then examine them. Look, first, for the ace of hearts. If it figures among the seven, your greatest strokes of good fortune will come on the day indicated by the row to which the ace belongs. Thus, if it is at the end of the second row, all your great enterprises should be conducted on Mondays.

But if the ace of hearts is not present among the seven, look for the King of Hearts and, failing him, the Queen of Hearts. Should neither of these be turned up, continue down the suit of hearts and follow on with clubs, diamonds and, lastly, spades, if needs be. Wherever the highest face card lies, according to the suits just named, there is the row which stands for your luckiest day.

It may be added that not only does this method indicate the lucky day, but the measure of luck, as well. Thus, if the ace of hearts turns up among the seven, the measure of luck is considerably great. It is even great if any heart is present. When a club ranks as the highest card, the amount of luck is still very satisfactory. It is moderate where a diamond takes priority, but if only spades are present the degree of luck is small.

# Your Future Luck

To know what the future has in store for you, persuade someone to act as your seer. This person should possess qualities as unlike your own as possible. Thus, if your eyes are blue, the seer's should be any colour but blue. In the matter of hair, complexion, height, build, temperament and occupation, you must, also, be as widely different as possible, but a difference of sex is not required.

Having selected a suitable seer, take a pack of playing cards and sort it into two heaps, the first containing all the court cards, and the second the number cards. For this purpose, the ace is considered a number card.

Now, match yourself with a suitable court card, as follows :

(a) If you possess brown hair of any shade, your match is the King or Queen of Clubs, according to whether you are a man or lady.

(*b*) If you possess golden hair, it is the King or Queen of Hearts.

(*c*) If you possess auburn hair of any shade, it is the King or Queen of Diamonds.

(*d*) If you possess black or grey hair, it is the King or Queen of Spades.

That done, take your matching card and place it in the pack containing all the number cards. This you must do yourself; but when you have shuffled as much as you think fit, hand the cards to the seer, who also shuffles them. It is important that both you and your friend perform the operation.

The next step is done entirely by the seer. He or she takes the pack, face downwards and turns the cards over, one by one, using the right hand for the purpose. None of the cards need be noted until the matching card is reached : then the one that immediately follows it is placed aside. Following this, the seer continues to turn over the cards until two more are uncovered of the same suit as the one set aside.

Now the three cards are placed in a line, in the order in which they came to light, and they are read according to the following clues :

## CLUBS

*Ace*—A dark person will enter your life ; dark in colouring, but not in colour.

*Two*—There is single blessedness in store for you. Probably you will prefer this, as you are hardly the person to put aside your own desires and subject them to the will of another.

*Three*—You will encounter troubles and bear them with fortitude.

*Four*—Your nature is not a quarrelsome one, yet you are fated to experience many unpleasant differences. You will overcome them all, however.

*Five*—You will make many friends ; but you will not keep any one for long.

*Six*—You will suddenly come upon a wonderful piece of luck ; it will be far in excess of your fair share.

*Seven*—There is happiness awaiting you, but it will not spring out of riches.

*Eight*—You will rise in the world and success will be yours.

*Nine.*—Your activities will take you in paths that will call for considerable courage and deep thinking.

*Ten*—You will be no " stay-at-home." You will experience a very full and busy life.

## HEARTS

*Ace*—You will rejoice in a fireside of your own, where you will be content to remain. Outside attractions will mean very little to you.

*Two*—The call of distant lands will urge you to leave home and friends, and seek your fortunes in the uttermost parts of the earth.

*Three*—Yours is to be a life of wealth and plenty. See to it that you gain happiness as well.

*Four*—Bliss and contentment are the greatest comforts of life. They will be yours, in abundance, and they will not be long in coming.

*Five*—There are signs that you will miss opportunities. While fate is knocking, you will be dreaming of things that really do not matter.

*Six*—You are about to disagree violently with somebody. Make quite sure that you are in the right before you assert your opinions.

*Seven*—A fortunate incident is about to occur which will give you considerable advantage in the work you have in hand.

*Eight*—The cards point to " wedding-bells." They may be for you, but if your married life is already planned, they are certainly for some dear friend.

*Nine*—There are regrets awaiting you. Act as you think most upright and they will not be too serious.

*Ten*—Have you drifted away from someone whom you should devoutly treasure—perhaps only in mind ? There is going to be a happy reunion.

## DIAMONDS

*Ace*—One of your friends is not as faithful as outward appearances suggest. Beware.

*Two*—Those difficulties, which are a source of worry to you. will be swept away shortly.

*Three*—Someone with a light complexion is about to enter your life. Welcome this person with all your might.

*Four*—Your passage through life will be a succession of ups and downs. Laugh at the worries and make the most of the good times.

*Five*—You are to be famous and your name will be known far and wide.

*Six*—If single blessedness is your present state, there are signs that it will not be long before a change occurs.

*Seven*—You will not be content to remain at your present level of life. Your ambitions will help you to climb high.

*Eight*—Fortune is about to knock at your door. Do not let it go away unanswered. It will knock lightly, but none the less definitely.

*Nine*—You are going to sustain a loss ; do not let it grieve you too heavily.

*Ten*—What has happened, has happened. You are going to enter upon a more even and happy phase of life.

## SPADES

*Ace*—You are to be beset with a spell of bad fortune. It will only remain for a time, however.

*Two*—Your kindly nature will be recognised by others and you will lose nothing by being generous.

*Three*—You will be blessed by a family or, if such exists already, it will be the means of much happiness to you.

*Four*—There are signs that you are fickle and that, in the long run, you will gain no happiness from this doubtful quality.

*Five*—A messenger will bring you ill-news.

*Six*—You are apt to put too high a price on riches. Remember that money is not everything.

*Seven*—To the unattached, there is a proposal looming on the horizon. To the married, a flirtation.

*Eight*—Depend on your friends and be loyal to them. They will help you in difficult times.

*Nine*—Misfortunes are about to strew your path. With diligence it will be possible to avoid the worst of them.

*Ten*—You have only to ask and your wishes will be gratified abundantly.

It should be noted that of the three cards, the first to be selected is the weakest and the third the strongest. Thus, if the reading of any card appears to be in direct variance with that of another, the second will outweigh the first, and the third will have a similar effect on the second.

# What Luck Will Attend You During The Week?

This is a very old method, used by fortune-tellers to determine how you will fare during the week that starts to-morrow. Under the heading, "Your Luck," you are told how to decide on your matching card. First, find this card and place it, face upwards, on the table : then, shuffle the remainder of the pack and, having cut with the left hand, deal off the top seven cards. Place these in a ring round the matching card, faces down.

Next, take seven cards at random from any part of the pack without looking at them. Place these cards on the original seven, one on each. Allow fate to determine how you pair-off the cards and do not set them down in any order of rotation—just put them one here and one there, until the seven pairs are formed.

Now, decide which pair shall stand for to-morrow—you can choose any pair you like, but if you happen to know any-thing of the value of the cards the whole of the spell will fail. Having decided on the pair that stands for to-morrow, the six following days continue round the circle in a clockwise fashion.

All the preliminaries being completed, you may turn over the cards and look at them.

*Two Hearts*, making a pair, stand for a day of considerable good fortune.

*One Heart* and one Club suggest almost as much good fortune.

*One Heart* and one Diamond are still fortunate.

*One Heart* and one Spade are mediumly fortunate.

*Two Clubs* are a sign of good fortune.

*One Club* and one Diamond are mediumly fortunate.

*One Club* and one Spade are moderate.

*Two Diamonds* are moderate.

*One Diamond* and one Spade are fair.

*Two Spades* are unlucky.

# YOUR LUCKY AND UNLUCKY NUMBERS

## MARRIAGE HARMONY AND NUMEROLOGY

## Numerology To Assist Your Fortune

Everybody is blessed with a number of their own and, if that number can be found and acted upon, considerable advantages must be derived. First of all let us tell you what your number is. Suppose you were born on the 15th day of the 11th month of the year 1907. Your number is found by reducing all these figures to their one basic figure. Thus

The 15th day $= 1 + 5 = 6$
The 11th month $= 1 + 1 = 2$
The year 1907 $= 1 + 9 + 0 + 7 = 17$
But 17, itself, must be reduced, thus, $1 + 7 = 8$

Altogether, you have $6 + 2 + 8 = 16$ and, as all two or more figured numbers must be reduced to a one-figured number, the 16 becomes $1 + 6 = 7$. Thus, if you were born on November 15, 1907, your fate number is 7.

But, of course, you were not born on this day in November, 1907, or you were hardly likely to be. So, put down your own birth date and find out, exactly as we have done, what your fate number is.

Once you have done that you will naturally ask how you can use it to advantage. The answer is simple. You are about to be married, you are applying for a post, you are thinking of starting on some large enterprise, it may be anything that concerns you greatly. Just jot down the date of this event and reduce it to its basic figure. If your fate number and that of the event are the same, you may be assured that great good will come of it. Perhaps the two figures are not the same. Can you make them so? Naturally, you cannot alter your own personal number; that is fixed for ever; but you may be able to shift the date of the event a day or two

backwards or forwards, and so make the two agree. In this way, you are using the science of numerology and applying it to your own good.

There is one thing more to be said. Just as you have a favourable number (your fate number) so you may have an unfavourable one. As has been hinted, numerology takes account of the numbers one to nine. Now, if you subtract your favourable number from nine, the answer provides the unfavourable number. It is on dates reducing themselves to this number that you should refrain, most assiduously, from undertaking any new or important enterprise.

In the case where a person's good number is, itself, nine, there can be no remainder when nine is subtracted from nine. Such people are, indeed, fortunate. They have no number that needs avoiding.

# The Numeral Alphabet

Now, each of the letters of the alphabet possesses a numeral value of its own and several are equal; the letters and their equivalents run thus:

| | | | |
|---|---|---|---|
| 1. | A | J | S |
| 2 | B | K | T |
| 3 | C | L | U |
| 4 | D | M | V |
| 5 | E | N | W |
| 6 | F | O | X |
| 7 | G | P | Y |
| 8 | H | Q | Z |
| 9 | I | R | |

The theory that each of us vibrates harmoniously or the reverse to one particular number is a very fascinating one, and may be discovered in the following manner.

*Names and Surnames.*—To find the value of any names or surnames, put the figures above or below each letter, as, for instance, take

| M | A | R | Y | | W | O | O | D | M | A | N |
|---|---|---|---|---|---|---|---|---|---|---|---|
| 4 | 1 | 9 | 7 | | 5 | 6 | 6 | 4 | 4 | 1 | 5 |

These added together total 52 (52 = 5 + 2 = 7).

Those contemplating marriage will find it an interesting study to discover by means of the above values whether

their nomenclatures are harmonious or the reverse, and herewith is a chart which will assist them in their decision :

Names vibrating to

<blockquote>

1 disagree with 6 and 7

3   ,,     ,, 4 and 7

4   ,,     ,, 3 and 5

5   ,,     ,, 2, 4 and 7

9   ,,     ,, 7

</blockquote>

whilst

<blockquote>

1 possesses attraction for 4 and 8

2     ,,        ,,    ,, 7 and 9

3     ,,        ,,    ,, 5, 6 and 9

4     ,,        ,,    ,, 1 and 8

5 and 6 ,,        ,,    ,, 3 and 9

7     ,,        ,,    ,, 2 and 6

8     ,,        ,,    ,, 1 and 4

9     ,,        ,,    ,, 2, 3 and 6

</blockquote>

# The Luck Of Numbers

Every number has its position in the scale of luck ; some are decidedly fortunate, others are quite the reverse. Odd numbers, as a rule, are considered more lucky than even, and most people, without knowing exactly why, pin their faith to Seven, which from time immemorial has been regarded as the perfect, spiritual, or magic number, since our lives are divided up into the seven ages of man.

Seven years form a cycle, and after a spell of sorrow, loss, and trouble, one somehow expects one's luck to change, and to expect that the one cycle may be succeeded by another more pleasant and prosperous, by way of compensation.

**No. 1** is regarded as among the strongest and most powerful of numbers. It stands for strength, boldness, activity, creative and inventive faculty, masculinity and directing powers. Its defects are limited vision, petulance, selfishness, officiousness and a tendency to enforce the individual's own ideas on others.

**No. 2** is distinctly opposed to No. 1, for it is feminine and receptive, and vibrates more to the heart than the mind ; it is supposed to be the ideal number for doctors, dentists,

mothers and nurses. It betokens quiet, calm, a restful influence, and it radiates charm, affection and a love of peace.

**No. 3** is considered to be the joy-giving numeral. It spells " cheerio," is typical of happiness, merriment, good cheer, pleasure, inspiration, even ecstasy. It influences literature, journalism, acting, public speaking, dancing, singing, music, painting, and is regarded as the numeral of declaration, expression and enunciation.

**No. 4,** like No. 1, is creative, but in a crude and limited sense. It is also physical, being pugnacious, material, greedy, acquiring and loving wealth simply for wealth's sake.

**No. 5** is regarded as unlucky and dual in character, being optimistic as well as pessimistic, constructive and destructive, depressed and cheerful. It has been regarded as unlucky, but has outlived the reputation, although not a tendency, for fickleness and inconsistency.

**No. 6** corresponds in various ways to No. 2, and is preeminently the marriage number. It is associated with peace, happiness, optimism, and strength. It is universal rather than personal in its scope, affects financial undertakings adversely, but is a good influence in matters artistic, philanthropic and physical.

**No. 7,** according to this up-to-date science, is not exactly lucky. It is more mysterious and obscure, and not the best number for starting any industrial scheme or pet project, as regards health and physical well-being. It is an important numeral, but it belongs more to the ascetic, the stoic and the mystic than the practical matter-of-fact man or woman's affairs.

**No. 8,** on the other hand, belongs to the latter class. It stands for excellence, for success in business and organisation, and, in a lesser degree, in science and intellectual concerns, but it does not typify achievement for the musician or the artist.

**No. 9** is the love number, and it also indicates universality, permanence, and steadfastness. Being a multiple of three, it is similar to that number, and is of practical help for speakers, actors, and singers.

Since it is the last of the numerals, its influence is as far removed as possible from that of One. It is looked upon as the origin of all vibrations, and anyone in whose name this

numeral is well-represented usually is well adapted for combating bravely all the obstacles which arise even in the path of the most successful.

Since there are only nine numbers, it follows that any two figures simply represent a union of these and they must be reduced to a unit.

For example, the number 16 is a combination of one and six, seven of six and one, $6 + 7 = 13$, which again stands for $1 + 3 = 4$, so that four is the value of the compound number and so on.

# THE COLOUR THAT BRINGS YOU LUCK

It is a well-accredited fact that our thoughts are varying rates of vibration and each rate possesses its own colour or hue. Individually, therefore, we respond to one particular colour or colours which affects our circulation and our mental movements. We are, therefore, out of harmony with others, hence the reason that one feels happy and at peace with all the world in a certain frock and the reverse in another.

The ancients looked upon white as the reunion of the seven primitive colours. Priests of old, regarded as the repositories of sacred knowledge, were clothed in white, so that it has become the prevailing colour adopted by women, at least in the chief religious ceremonies of their life.

We array babies, brides, and the dead in white, since it denotes innocence, purity, chastity.

Black is the colour of sadness, gloom, and death. The old legend declared that Apollo turned the raven black because it had betrayed him, so his Satanic Majesty and his satellites are generally depicted in funeral-like garments.

Red, symbolic of fire, represents power, passion, and riches, and so the rulers of mankind arrayed themselves in robes of this resplendent hue, as did the executioners of old and the members of the Spanish Inquisition. It is the colour of physical feeling and ranges from the crimson hue seen by men in a fit of anger or passion to the delicate shell-pink of affection. The one is irritating to some; the latter denotes love, health, and pleasure, and is restful and soothing to most.

According to some psychologists, typists and others work far better in a room with red walls than any other, but they tire more readily than in a grey or yellowish-green room.

Orange is the colour of the Muses and of Hymen, the god of marriage. Brides, in the twilight of the world, wore veils, or flammeum, of this colour, hence the association in the minds of some with orange blossom and the nuptial rites.

Yellow, on the other hand, signified glory and fortune to the ancients. Now it is considered the sign of infidelity,

perfidy, or shame.  The early Christians, however, thinking it
reflected the rays of the sun, adjudged it to be the colour of
holiness and devotion, and draped the earliest images of St.
Peter in its golden hues.  It typifies force and energy and in
certain instances stimulating and healing qualities.

Green, the colour of springtime, is invariably associated with
youth and hope, and is regarded as invigorating, so that
up-to-date doctors are insisting on the walls of nursing homes
being distempered in this colour, in the best interests of their
patients.

A combination of violet and green is said to be an excellent
means of stimulating vague personalities.

Purple was the imperial colour worn by Roman emperors
and conquerors, and has always been associated with majesty,
power, and faith.

One of the seven primary colours, blue, has been termed
" Heaven's own colour."  It runs the gamut from the light
blue of intellectuals to the deep indigo of music.  It is the
pre-eminent colour in religion, art, and heraldry, and represents amongst other virtues, peace, piety, tranquillity,
a love of good works and divine contemplation.  As the
popular tint of the Virgin Mary's robes, it signifies modesty.
It is believed to be the most powerful and soothing of colours ;
it calms angry passions, when red only irritates, and
psychologists advise women to wear blue in any tint when they
desire to placate a man or win a favour from a member of
the opposite sex.

## Your Own Colour

So much for colours, their effects and their meanings.
Now, as to how they influence you personally.  It may be
that you have found some particular shade to be associated
with your luck, though it is more usual for a colour to go
hand-in-hand with your misfortunes.  We know of several
people who would not dream of wearing green, because a slice
of ill-luck has overtaken them whenever they wore such a
dress, in the past.  And as with green, so with every other
colour :  there are people who have found them unfortunate.

If you have not noticed which colours to avoid and which
to favour, it will be useful to point out that the signs of the
Zodiac are each associated with definite colours.  Therefore,

if you employ the particular colour of the Zodiac sign under which you were born, you may be sure that the fates are working for you. Here are these colours :

| *Born between* | *Colour to choose* |
|---|---|
| Dec. 22nd and Jan. 20th. (Capricorn) | Black, dark brown. |
| Jan. 21st and Feb. 19th. (Aquarius) | Black, blue. |
| Feb. 20th and March 20th. (Pisces) | Blue, purple, mauve. |
| March 21st and April 19th. (Aries) | Scarlet. |
| April 20th and May 20th. (Taurus) | Blue, and any colour incorporating blue. |
| May 21st and June 21st. (Gemini) | Yellow, green, orange. |
| June 22nd and July 22nd. (Cancer) | Green, grey. |
| July 23rd and August 22nd. (Leo) | Yellow, gold. |
| Aug. 23rd and Sept. 22nd. (Virgo) | Brown, grey. |
| Sept. 23rd and Oct. 23rd. (Libra) | Brown, green, blue. |
| Oct. 24th and Nov. 22nd. (Scorpio) | Dark red, crimson. |
| Nov. 23rd and Dec. 21st. (Sagittarius) | Purple. |

# THE STONE YOU SHOULD WEAR FOR LUCK

There are several ways of deciding which stone will bring you luck, but the most usual is to wear the one that is associated with the month in which your birthday falls. The verses of poetry, set out below, will help you to find out your own particular stone, according to this method, if you do not already know.

JANUARY

> By her who in this month was born
> No gem save Garnets should be worn—
> They will insure her constancy,
> True friendship, and fidelity.

FEBRUARY

> The February born shall find
> Sincerity and peace of mind,
> Freedom from passion and from care
> If they the Amethyst will wear.

MARCH

> Who on this world of ours their eyes
> In March first open shall be wise,
> In days of peril, firm and brave,
> And wear a Bloodstone to their grave.

APRIL

> She who from April dates her years—
> Diamonds should wear lest bitter tears
> For vain repentance flow ; this stone
> Emblem of innocence is known.

MAY

> Who first beholds the light of day
> In spring's sweet, flowery month of May,
> And wears an Emerald all her life
> Shall be a loved and happy wife.

JUNE

> Who comes with summer to this earth,
> And owes to June her hour of birth,
> With ring of Agate on her hand
> Can health, wealth, and long life command.

19

### July

The glowing Ruby shall adorn
Those who in warm July are born,
Then will they be exempt and free
From love's doubt and anxiety.

### August

Wear a Sardonyx or for thee
No conjugal felicity—
The August born without this stone,
'Tis said, must live unloved and lone.

### September

A maiden born when autumn leaves
Are rustling in the September breeze,
A Sapphire on her brow should bind,
'Twill cure diseases of the mind.

### October

October child is born for woe,
And life's vicissitudes must know;
But lay an Opal on her breast
And hope will lull those woes to rest.

### November

Who first comes to this world below
With drear November's fog and snow
Should prize the Topaz's amber hue,
Emblem of friends and lovers true.

### December

If cold December gave you birth,
The month of snow and ice and mirth,
Place on your hand a Turquoise blue,
Success will bless whate'er you do.

The significance of these stones is, briefly, as follows :

*Agate.*—This was supposed in days of old to call down the favour of the gods, and since it contains pretty markings like trees and mosses, it is considered specially good for gardeners, foresters, farmers and all people who grow things. It endows the wearer with love and friendship.

*Amethyst.*—This is pre-eminently the lover's stone, as it was dedicated to St. Valentine, their patron saint. It signifies true love and fidelity, and brings the best of luck to those born in February.

*Bloodstone.*—It is the emblem of courage, and soldiers of old wore it in battle, believing it had the power to stop bleeding.

It is more suitable for men than women, but whoever wears it has a talisman for warding off disease and accidents.

*Diamond.*—This stone was deemed to be the most powerful of any, it being a symbol of the sun and of invincible fire. It expelled fear and promoted courage. To it was attributed wisdom, insight, innocence and joy, especially when worn on the left side.

*Emerald.*—According to an old legend, if this gem were bestowed by a lover, it only retained its exquisite depth of colour as long as both remained faithful, but it grew dull and pale if either tired of each other.

*Garnet.*—This is a form of Ruby, but less red in colour and sometimes even pink. Its special duties are to ward off diseases in which inflammation plays a part. It provides the wearer with a cheerful nature and a healthy life.

*Opal.*—This beautiful stone is supposed to change colour with the emotions of the wearer, flushing with love and pleasure, and paling in the presence of foes. It stands, mainly, for hope, though those coming under its sway possess foresight and prophetic powers. At one time, it was looked upon as an ill-omen, but whatever reputation it had in this direction has now disappeared entirely.

*Ruby.*—It is well to remember that this stone need not be blood-red, as there are specimens which are green, purple, and even black. It is said to drive away ghosts and sadness, to inspire confidence and bring good fortune.

*Sapphire.*—All blue stones are lucky to lovers, since they are the colour of Venus, the goddess of love. To the sapphire is attributed the powers of providing a peaceful influence, love, hope and joy ; but all its virtues perish in the possession of an evil-doer.

*Sardonyx.*—Its chief powers are those of preserving the wearer from the dangers of snakes and other venomous creatures.

*Topaz.*—This stone wards off attacks of asthma, chest troubles, rheumatic complaints, and even brain diseases, according to the ancients, who valued it highly for its medicinal powers.

*Turquoise.*—This stone varies with the mood of its owner, and is supposed to fade when its possessor is about to die. It has the property of watching over people and preventing them from falls, which might endanger their lives.

# THE
# WHEEL OF DESTINY

We have taken this trial of fortune telling from an ancient manuscript. You are required to hold a sharp-pointed instrument in the hand, to shut your eyes, and then to make your decision by bringing the point on to the fateful wheel. On opening your eyes, note the number or letter chosen, and read the explanation in the list below. You are allowed one reading, each, in the white and black spaces.

LOVE

1. Many lovers.
2. One sincere lover, one false one.
3. A mere flirtation.
4. A senseless jest.
5. A lover who has not courage to speak his mind.
6. You love and are not beloved again—so banish the flame.

## COURTSHIP

1. The lover is sincere.
2. No wedlock is intended.
3. They are wavering in love.
4. A long courtship, to end in nothing.
5. It will end in marriage.
6. A sudden break.

## MARRIAGE

1. Happy, and of long duration.
2. Short, but prosperous and peaceful.
3. Not so soon as you expect, but happy in itself.
4. Not so happy in the end as the beginning promiseth.
5. A separation before death.
6. A paradise on earth awaits you in this respect.

## OFFSPRING

1. They will surround your table like olive-branches.
2. Several in number,—some as roses to you, and some will prove thorns.
3. One at most.
4. Not many.
5. One amongst your children will raise you to affluence, —they will all prove acceptable.
6. Other people's children will add to your anxieties.

## KINDRED

1. They will enrich you.
2. They will impoverish you.
3. They will exalt you.
4. They will degrade you.
5. Some of your kindred will leave you a valuable remembrance.
6. A death in the family.

## TRADE

1. You will never be indebted to it in your own person.
2. You will suddenly embark in it.
3. You will form a friendship with a trader.
4. You will lose by trade.
5. You will enter into partnership.
6. You will get rich by commerce.

## FORTUNE

1. Changes every seven years will occur to you.
2. A steady life.
3. Sudden riches.
4. Fatal extravagance.
5. False promises will undo your peace.
6. A sudden fall and a great rise will mark your life.

## SPECULATION

1. Success in the lottery.
2. Never speculate.
3. Chance luck.
4. Fortunate at cards.
5. You will be lucky at ventures in trade.
6. Luck in a wager to come.

## THE POINTS

*A*, a letter.  *B*, a reproof.  *C*, a loss.
*D*, a gain.  *E*, new apparel.  *F*, a gift.
*G*, a journey.  *X*, a disappointment.  *Y*, a feast.

1. A comfortable hour.   2. A change.
3. Bad news.   4. Good tidings.
5. A voyage.   6. A present of money.
7. A valentine.   8. A gift to wear.
9. A present for which you will pay dearly.
10. You have acted recently in an unworthy manner.
15. You are about to lose something.
17. Great joy is yours.

Other numbers are fortunate.
Crosses under a figure emphasise the reading.

# LUCKY MARRIAGES

According to the lore of the ancients, there is a whole host of do's and don'ts for those about to marry, should they desire that good fortune attends their nuptials.

Long before the eventful day, the bride must see to it that she does not transgress any of the rules laid down by Fate, if she hopes for a married life of unalloyed bliss. First,

she must make a large portion of her trousseau, or her luck will be out : but, curiously enough, she must on no account make the bridal gown. And here, let it be said that the girls who sew it should enclose one of their own hairs in the folds, if they, too, wish to be married soon.

## The Lucky Colour

The old tradition demands that the bride must wear

Something old, something new,
Something borrowed, something blue.

White is not necessarily a bride's only wear nowadays. Custom has sanctioned almost every colour of late years, save the fateful green, which is the fairies' colour, and they punish any mortal who has the temerity to wear it on her wedding-day.

## The Lucky Wedding-Day

MONDAY for health,
TUESDAY for wealth,
    WEDNESDAY the best day of all ;
THURSDAY for losses,
FRIDAY for crosses,
    And SATURDAY no luck at all.

Most people confess to a dislike of Monday and Friday, the latter because of what happened so long ago on the first Good Friday.

The majority of women favour Wednesday and Saturday, and the former is one of the most popular of wedding-days, notably in June (which takes its name from the goddess Juno, the protector of women), and particularly if it should happen to be the fourth of that month.

## Good Omens

Should the bride be awakened on her wedding morn by the song of a bird, even though it be only the chirping of a city sparrow, she may accept that as a good augury, also if she discovers a spider in the folds of her dress, for that means she will always have plenty. She must not break anything, especially a mirror, or lose the heel of a shoe. She must not forget to feed the family cat. If a black cat rubs against her, then she is likely to be specially lucky. Any jewels are lucky except pearls, but this superstition has almost died out.

If she glance into the mirror as she is bound to do on such an auspicious occasion, she must add something to her toilet, even if it be only her gloves.

When she leaves her home to be married, then she must re-enter by the same door, and the same holds good regarding the church. She must always step into the building right foot first to ensure luck ; and if she stumbles or falls the superstitious will prophesy evil.

If a bride sees her bridegroom before he catches a glimpse of her, she will dominate him all her life.

If bride and bridegroom smile at each other as they meet at the altar, it augurs well for their future happiness ; also, if they happen to look into a mirror together directly after the ceremony.

A bride is not supposed to weep before marriage, but she may do so to her heart's content after the actual ceremony, and thus prove that she is no witch, as the latter could only shed three tears from her left eye !

If the bride see a lamb, a dove, a spider, or a toad on her way to church, then these are emblems of good luck, but it is reckoned as a very bad omen if she should encounter a funeral party or if a pig should cross the road in front of the carriage or motor.

The bridal bouquet should be broken up and tossed amongst the bridesmaids and girl friends, and whoever catches these is expected to wed very soon.

On changing her wedding toilette for her going-away gown, a bride should remove all the pins, and either throw them away or toss them to her friends, otherwise bad luck may attend her.

## The Bridegroom's Luck

Few superstitions concern themselves with the conduct of the bridegroom on these occasions, as long as he does not see his bride in her bridal attire before he meets her at the altar, let his hat fall, drop the ring, or only put it partially on his bride's finger. If she has to assist him to do so, then he may expect to be ruled by her in future. He should fee the clergyman with an odd sum of money, carry a small mascot in his pocket, and on no account must he turn back for anything, after the wedding journey is once started.

## Throwing An Old Shoe

The custom of throwing an old shoe after the happy pair, as they leave for the honeymoon, is not altogether one to bring luck, but it is so universally done that no bride nor bridegroom would feel entirely satisfied were that part of the ceremony forgotten.

The rice and the confetti is different. They are thrown in order to bestow a life of plenty on the newly-married couple.

# The Home Coming

Brides should be generally carried across the threshold of their new home. In Scotland, the mother-in-law broke a cake of shortbread, in Ireland an oaten cake, over her head in token of an augury of plenty. In some cases the newly-made wife was invested with a poker and shovel and tongs, in recognition of authority.

Another old custom consists of two of the bride's bridesmaids or girl friends meeting her at the door. One carries a towel or table napkin which is placed over the bride's head, while the other pours over it a quantity of bread and cakes, which is eagerly grabbed by the children who have gathered round the door.

In the North of England, the maid pours a kettle of hot water over the doorstep to ensure that another wedding will take place ere long from the same house, and the Slavs deluge a bridegroom's head with beer, as an expression of good feeling and for luck.

# The Bridesmaid's Luck

The popular girl who is asked time and again to act as bridesmaid should refuse in her own interests, since according to an old saw : " Three times a bridesmaid, never a bride."

# Bygone Beliefs

Such a subject as marriage has, naturally, given rise to a good many curious beliefs in bygone ages. Some are worth recording here. The first is a recipe for marriage :

" Let three, five, or seven young women stand in a circle, and draw a card out of a bag ; she who gets the highest card will be married first, whether she be at the present time maid, wife, or widow ; and she who has the lowest, has the longest time to stay till the wedding-day ; she who draws the ace of spades will never bear the name of wife ; and she who has the nine of hearts in this trial will have one lover too many, to her sorrow."

We wonder how many maidens were sufficiently enthusiastic to complete the requirements of the following scheme for getting information about their future husbands :

" St. Agnes' Day falls on the 21st of January ; prepare yourself by a twenty-four hours' fast, taking nothing but pure spring water, beginning at midnight on the 21st ; then go to bed, and sleep by yourself ; and do not mention what you are trying to anyone or it will break the spell ; lie on your left side, and repeat these lines three times :

> St. Agnes, be a friend to me,
> In the gift I ask of thee ;
> Let me this night my husband see—

and you will dream of your future spouse ; if you see more men than one in your dream, you will wed two or three times, but if you sleep and dream not, you will never marry."

This suggestion was probably a great deal more popular than the previous one :

" Purchase three small keys, each at a different place, and, going to bed, tie them together with your garter, and place them in your left-hand glove, with a small flat dough-cake,

on which you have pricked the first letters of your sweetheart's name; put them in your bosom when you retire to rest; if you are to have that young man you will dream of him, but not else."

Another bedtime suggestion :

" Lay under your pillow a prayer-book opened at the matrimonial service, bound round with the garters you wore that day, and a sprig of myrtle on the page that says, *With this ring I thee wed*, and your dream will be ominous."

The following is certainly interesting :

" Try this on the third day of any month between September and March. Let any number of young women not exceeding nine, and minding that there is an odd one in the company, and each string nine acorns on a separate string, or as many acorns as there are females, but not more ; wrap them round a long stick of wood, and place it in the fire, just as the clock strikes twelve at night ; say not a word, but sit round the fire till all the acorns are consumed, then take out the ashes, and retire to bed almost directly, repeating :

> May love and marriage be the theme,
> To visit me in this night's dream ;
> Gentle Venus, be my friend,
> The image of my lover send ;
> Let me see his form and face,
> By a symbol or a sign,
> Cupid, forward my design."

# YOUR MARRIAGE MONTH

Every single woman and most men are interested to know in which month of the year they are to be married. Unfortunately for them, it is not a matter that can be decided by the Fates. What the Fates can do is to state the month in which a person should marry in order to ensure the greatest happiness and good fortune.

The Signs of the Zodiac

Would you know, if you are single, when you ought to marry? Then, take a pin in the left hand, shut your eyes and banish everything from your thoughts except matters relating to your future husband or wife. Revolve the pin seven times—three in a clockwise direction, three in the reverse sense, and once in whichever way you please. Finally, rest the point of the pin on the diagram of the Signs of the

Zodiac. Note in which section the point rests and then seek the clue to your marriage month in the following list :

| 1. | The sign being Aries, you should marry in April. |
| 2. | ,, ,, Taurus ,, ,, May |
| 3. | ,, ,, Gemini ,, ,, June |
| 4. | ,, ,, Cancer ,, ,, July |
| 5. | ,, ,, Leo ,, ,, August |
| 6. | ,, ,, Virgo ,, ,, September |
| 7. | ,, ,, Libra ,, ,, October |
| 8. | ,, ,, Scorpio ,, ,, November |
| 9. | ,, ,, Sagittarius ,, ,, December |
| 10. | ,, ,, Capricorn ,, ,, January |
| 11. | ,, ,, Aquarius ,, ,, February |
| 12. | ,, ,, Pisces ,, ,, March |

Although it is accurate enough for most purposes to say that Aries represents April, and the same with all the other months, yet it is not quite correct. Aries begins on March 21 and ends on April 19. Thus, when a month is stated above, reckon the final ten days of the previous month and rule out the last ten days of the month mentioned. (Example : Gemini rules from May 21 to June 20.)

One other matter. What if the pin engages the point in the black spaces, surrounding the signs ? We would rather leave the reader to guess the meaning of such a happening.

# THE MAGIC TABLETS

The following method of telling fortunes has been in existence close on a thousand years, though slight emendations have been made so that it will serve for modern conditions.

The rules are that, first, you place the little finger on any letter by chance, in the first tablet (it is better to do it with a pin and while your eyes are shut). Then, you refer in the second tablet to the letter so found, and note the number under it. Thirdly, refer to this number in the following oracle. Thus, you arrive at your fortune.

### TABLET No. 1

```
        A   C   D
      Z   F   X   L
    N   A   P   N   O   C
  D   L   Q   Y   R   S   T
  E   H   G   L   K   V   W
T   S   V   A   N   M   C   D
  P   O   R   B   W   X   A
C   H   C   I   X   F   G   S
  B   H   L   L   W   V   U
  O   F   T   S   V   D   L
      M   X   Z   A   B
      W   B   B   L   M
      O   N   Q   S   Y
```

### TABLET No. 2

|    | A  | B  | C  |    |
|----|----|----|----|----|
|    | 25 | 15 | 5  |    |
| D  | E  | F  | H  | G  |
| 14 | 16 | 6  | 13 | 7  |
| I  | K  | L  | M  | N  |
| 18 | 8  | 17 | 1  | 9  |
| O  | P  | Q  | R  | S  |
| 10 | 22 | 3  | 12 | 23 |
| T  | V  | U  | W  |    |
| 19 | 2  | 24 | 4  |    |
|    | X  | Y  | Z  |    |
|    | 20 | 21 | 11 |    |

# THE ORACLE

## (a) GOOD FORTUNE

**1.** If this number is fixed upon by a man, it insures him, if single, a homely wife, but rich ; if married, an access of riches, numerous children and an old age. To a lady, the faithfulness of her lover, and a speedy marriage.

**3.** Very good fortune, sudden prosperity, great respect from high personages, and a letter bringing important news.

**7.** This number, to a single woman, shows a handsome, rich, and constant husband ; if married, a faithful partner, of a good family, as she must know she has married above her condition ; to a man the same.

**8.** This is a general good sign, and your present expectations will be fulfilled, and you have some on the anvil.

**9.** If a married man or woman draws this, if under fifty, let them not despair of a young family ; to the single, very sudden marriage.

**10.** A friend has crossed the sea, and will bring home some riches, by which the parties will be much benefited.

**12.** An uncommon number belonging to scriptural signs, and shows the party will have success in all their undertakings.

**15.** No doubt but the chooser is very poor, and thought insignificant, but let friends assist him or her, as they are much favoured.

**16.** A very sudden journey, with a pleasant fellow-traveller, and the result of the journey will be generally beneficial to your family.

**18.** A sudden acquaintance with the opposite sex, which will be opposed ; but the party should persevere, as it will be to his or her advantage.

**21.** A letter of importance will arrive, announcing the death of a relation for whom you have no very great respect, but who has left you a legacy.

**22.** Be very prudent in your conduct, as this number is very precarious, and much depends on yourself : it is generally good.

**23.** A very accomplished young woman will be the wife of the man who choses this number.

**24.** Let the chooser of this number persevere : all his or her schemes are good and must succeed.

# THE ORACLE

## (b) BAD FORTUNE

2. Shows the loss of a friend, bad success at law, loss of money, unfaithfulness of lovers, and a bad partner.

4. A letter announcing the loss of money.

5. The man who draws this number, let him examine his moles, and he will find, I know, more about him than he imagines.

6. Very bad success; you may expect generally not to succeed in any of your undertakings.

11. I should rather suspect the fidelity of your husband or wife, if married; if single, you are shockingly deceived.

13. You want to borrow money, and you hope you will have it; but you will be deceived.

14. The old man you have depended upon is going to be married, and will become a father.

17. You have mixed with this company, and pretend to despise our tablets, but you rely much upon them, and you may depend on it that you will be brought to disgrace.

19. Look well to those who owe you money, if ever so little: a letter of abuse may be expected.

20. A drunken partner, and bad success in trade: the party will never be very poor, but always unhappy.

25. The man or woman who chooses this unlucky number, let them look well to their conduct: justice, though slow is sure to overtake the wicked.

# TALISMANS AND MASCOTS FOR LUCK

People will tell you that the wearing of mascots is no longer a habit and that, in these enlightened days, nobody puts any faith in them. But is this actually so? Cannot the horse-shoe be seen hanging in all sorts of places and does not the average motorist carry some mystic charm on the bonnet? What of the bouquet of white flowers which the blushing bride takes with her to the altar and the ring which her future husband gave her when they became engaged? No; the fact is that mascots are believed in to-day just as much as they were a thousand years ago. If the truth were known, we should probably find that more faith is placed in them now than ever before.

For this reason it will be interesting to consult the following alphabetical list of mascots and charms, and many readers may be inclined to select one or other of them for their own personal use.

ABRACADABRA.—The ancients inscribed this mystic word on a slip of parchment and fastened it around their necks. So worn, the individual was supposed to be proof against evil spirits and, notably, against the dreaded evil eye. The word had to be written in this form:

ABRACADABRA  
BRACADABR  
RACADAB  
ACADA  
CAD  
A  

It will be seen that the word can be read along the top line and also down and up the two sloping sides.

ACORN.—Throughout the history of England, since the days of the Norman Conquest, it has been a custom for people to carry a dried acorn, in the belief that it will endow them with youth. It was also supposed to have the effect of making a wayward lover relent and return to his or her jilted companion.

ANCHOR.—People who lived on or near the sea have long regarded the anchor as a symbol of hope, safety and good fortune.

ANGLE.—An angle, shaped like the letter L, was supposed by the Greeks to give learning and understanding to those of scholarly habits.

ARROW-HEADS have served as charms ever since primitive days. The earliest were made of flint and were small enough to be suspended around the neck. Their chief use was to ward off the evil eye. Those that were found naturally shaped were considered to be far more efficacious than those artificially shaped.

AXES.—The ancients carved suitable pieces of stone to the shape of axe-heads and used them exactly as mentioned for arrow-heads. The only difference was that arrow-heads were invariably made of flints, while axe-heads were more likely to be carved out of an attractive stone which lent itself to polishing.

BADGER.—The tooth of a badger has long been considered to be a lucky mascot for card-players. The connection between such a tooth and cards is not clear, though the use has persisted almost since the time when cards originated.

The Bamboo and Serpent

BAMBOO AND SERPENT.—A very old talisman, often seen depicted in ancient documents, consists of a ring bearing a number of triangles. Lying on the ring is a serpent crossed with a stick of bamboo, which invariably bears seven knots.

The ring stands for eternity which, like the ring, never ends. The triangles on the ring are composed each of three sides, and thus symbolise the Trinity. The seven-knotted bamboo stood for the seven degrees of learning which had to be acquired by all who hoped to rank among the learned; while the serpent was an additional sign of wisdom. Thus, the talisman was worn by all who attempted to gain skill and knowledge of a high degree.

BANGLES.—Almost as old as the ring, the bangle is a symbol that the wearer becomes the "slave" of the person who provides the bangle.

BEADS, when worn by children, have long been supposed to protect them from the evil eye, and particularly from illnesses. Coral was considered to be the proper material.

BEES worked into jewellery and other ornaments for wearing purposes are supposed to be mascots which give the wearer remarkable powers of endurance, perseverance and commercial ability. They are specially potent in working for the good of those who deal in merchandise, and who are connected with buying and selling.

BELLS have the power of frightening away the evil spirits: thus, people carried small representations of them in order to be proof against evil and trouble. The tolling of a church bell is a custom that has grown out of this belief.

BLACK CATS are considered lucky because they were the pets of witches. If such an animal were badly treated, it would bring down the vengeance of the witches. Therefore, they were invariably treated kindly. It followed, then, that people went out of their way to collect black cats and lavish kindness on them in order to curry favour with the witches. Hence the idea that they are bringers of luck.

BULL.—Many people carry little replicas of bulls, especially their heads, in order to symbolise strength, power and determination—qualities which the ancients attributed to this animal.

CAUL.—The covering found on the head and face of some children when they are born is considered to be the most

reliable mascot in existence. Not only does it bring luck and good fortune to the baby born with it, but also to anyone who subsequently possesses it. Its powers for doing good are of a general character—it will bring luck in any and every emergency, though it is supposed to be remarkably efficacious in any matters connected with the sea or water. Thus, a possessor of a caul should not fear drowning.

CLOVER is lucky if possessed of four leaves. The poet has put this into verse :

> One leaf for fame,
> And one leaf for wealth,
> A third for a faithful lover,
> Yet another to bring you glorious health,
> Are all in a four-leaf clover.

COAL is lucky when found, but not if bought or acquired in the ordinary way. A whole year of good fortune is bestowed on the household, if a dark man carrying a piece of coal is the first person to cross the threshold after the Old Year has given place to the New.

CORNUCOPIA.—Otherwise called the Horn of Plenty, this mascot consists of a curved horn, out of which emerges an unlimited supply of fruit and flowers. The idea is that the contents of the horn are symbolical of plenty : thus to wear a replica of this device is to ensure an abundance of wealth and prosperity.

DOLPHIN.—This mythical creature of fish-like characteristics was attributed to Apollo, and has long been the particular mascot of those interested in music, literature and painting.

EVIL EYE.—Since earliest times, people have believed that the " evil eye " was watching them unceasingly in the hope of doing them some injury. Every ill and every trouble was thus ascribed to the " evil eye." To counteract its effects, individuals wore little polished stones or pieces of metal bearing a representation of the " evil eye," in the belief that one eye would frighten away the other.

EYE.—This amulet or charm represents the Sun, which is spoken of as " The Eye of Day," and is symbolical of the Supreme Intelligence, or the All-Seeing Eye of the Diety. From being a circle with a point in the centre, which de-notes the First Manifestation of the Divine Being, it was later made to take the form of an open eye, and as such

was in general use as an amulet to forfend against evils
of enchantment, enmity, and diseases of all kinds. A

The Eye

talisman, embodying the symbols of both
the Sun and Moon—i.e., the left eye and
the right eye together—was formed at
the new moon in Leo or Cancer, these
being the signs of the Sun and Moon,
when the Sun, being near the summer
solstice, has its greatest strength, which
it transfers to the Moon, so that a double
source of protection and strength is in-
voked by this combination. Its simple form is shown in
the diagram.

FISH.—The symbol of the fish has always been regarded
as a sign of increase and wealth, because of its remarkable
fertility, and even in these days it is seen cut out of mother-
of-pearl and used as a charm or pendant for good fortune.
In ancient days the worship of Dagon, i.e., the Sun Fish,
was prevalent among the Syrians, and may have given rise
to the conception of the Mermaid. The fish symbol is not
peculiar to the talismanic art of the Philistines, but has entered
into the rites of the Hebrews, who may have adopted it during
one of their lapses into idolatry. The name Dag is Hebrew
for fish, and as Dagon it is suggested that
the Sun was worshipped on its entry into
the sign Pisces.

HAND.—Many people carry a charm
which consists of a hand ; usually it
represents the hand of Fatima, who was
a daughter of Mohamet. The fingers
of the hand stand for the qualities of
Hospitality, Generosity, Strength and
Goodness, and it was supposed that
anyone who carried this charm would be
endowed with the virtues enumerated.

HEART.—To wear the heart as a mascot
is a relic of the Egyptian idea, which
was that people's hearts were to be
weighed at the resurrection and only
those proving satisfactory would be

The Hand of Fatima

accepted into Heaven. Later the heart became a symbol
of love, so that lovers give a mascot of this shape to each
other as a testimony of their affections.

HORSESHOE.—This is probably the most popular luck-bringer of all. To be effective, it should be suspended with the horns pointing upwards.

KEYS.—The Greek Key, which figures in so many patterns, symbolised life. A more usual rendering of the symbol shows it in a group of three. One key stood for love, a second for wealth, and a third for health. The keys were supposed to unlock the doors which led to these valuable qualities.

KNOTS.—A knot stands for the joining of two things, hence knots of various kinds have long been symbols valued by lovers. Everyone knows of " true lovers' knots."

LADYBIRDS.—These creatures are supposed to bring financial luck to those possessing them, but only as long as no harm is done to them. Accordingly, people wear imitation lady-birds, so that they may enjoy the luck without causing any harm to the creatures.

LYRE.—This musical instrument is associated with Apollo, and when worn as a mascot is supposed to provide the wearer with the qualities for which he has the greatest ambitions.

The Lyre Mascot

MODERN MASCOTS.—Of these there are several to which people pin their faith. There is Little Billiken and a host of others. No valid reason can be offered as to why any person

desirous of possessing a mascot should not originate a novelty of his own. The only requirement is that the possessor should endow it with his faith for it to prove a comfort and a bringer of luck.

OWL.—The owl is a bird symbolising knowledge and commonsense, in spite of a popular belief to the contrary. Thus, charms portraying this bird have long been worn by those interested in learning and study.

PENNIES bearing the date of a leap year are supposed to protect from harm people carrying them on their person.

PIGS.—Several people wear a broken pig as a charm ; i.e., the leg, tail, or snout has been purposely damaged. The idea is that the damage to the pig will swallow up any damage that might arise to you, while wearing it.

RING.—It is unnecessary to say much about rings, as most people understand their particular uses. Obviously, the significance is " eternity," as neither Heaven nor a ring has any ending.

SERPENTS.—These creatures have long been regarded as typical of wisdom, especially in the matter of healing. Therefore, charms shaped like serpents have been worn for a thousand years by those who wished to have great knowledge and freedom from disease.

SHAMROCK.—The Druids were the first to see in the shamrock a harbinger of good luck.

SWASTIKA.—The wheel and cross is a very ancient mascot. The word " swastika " comes from the Sanscrit and means " purveyor of good fortune." It is a tacit affirmation of the fact that we reap what we sow, and that present effects are the direct fruit of past causes. In this sense, it embodies the idea of the human soul, by cyclic peregrination and experience.

TAU.—This symbol is in universal use as a sacred emblem and is subjected to many variations of form. The simplest of these is the one formed by two straight lines, one being vertical and the other superimposed upon it horizontally. The popular belief is that it wards off almost every disease of the skin.


# Your Own Lucky Mascot

Very many people wear or carry mascots though, of course, they do not all tell you so. A mascot, on your person, if it

does no more, will give you assurance. It may help you to all manner of good things.

In choosing a mascot, many difficulties may arise and, likely enough, no individual specimen will make a hundred per cent. appeal to you. In such a case the proper thing to do is to fashion your own particular charm. Take a circle of cardboard, about an inch and a half or two inches in

Symbols used for Mascots

diameter, and draw on it just the symbols that your fancy dictates. Cover it in some of the transparent paper that is used for wrapping chocolate boxes and a hundred other things, and your little mascot will stand up to hard wear for a long time.

What symbols should you inscribe on your mascot ? That is a matter which you must decide entirely by yourself, but if you need inspirations, a glance through the pages of this book will surely give you ideas. On page 43, several charms have been drawn purposely with the object of helping you in your selection.

No. 1 is the swastika, which helps us to make our best efforts to succeed.

No. 2 is the crescent, associated with the new moon. It is a symbol conferring favours on things that are new, from newborn babes to new business enterprises.

No. 3 is the key which unlocks the door to love, wealth and health.

No. 4 reveals the most debatable of all numbers. Is it lucky or is it not ? More people believe it to be lucky than otherwise, but they do not argue about it as much as those who hold it in dishonour. Our opinion is that it is decidedly lucky.

No. 5 is the Tau which wards off disease, notably those which attack the surface of the body. Would you preserve your beauty, then the Tau will help you.

No. 6 is the scarab, which provides health and strength, and preserves people from peril.

No. 7 is an anchor, a symbol of hope, safety, and good fortune.

No. 8 is a curious figure : it is a symbol representing the spirit of the Moon, and all who pay homage to the Moon are supposed to be guided in choosing the right time for doing things of importance.

No. 9 is a dolphin, a mythical creature which watches over those who are interested in music, painting and literature.

# A TALISMAN TO SECURE ELOQUENCE

This Talisman should be made on a Wednesday. It is said to aid one in learning and public speaking, and should be worn by clergymen, auctioneers, politicians, etc.

# A TALISMAN FOR HEALTH

This should be made on a Sunday, and is said to be a wonderful preservative for Health, also curing diseases. All persons suffering should wear one : even when in health it is well to possess one.

# A TALISMAN FOR TRAVELLING
## BY LAND OR SEA

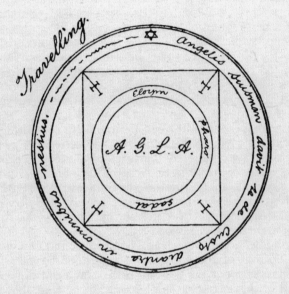

This Talisman should be made on a Monday, and is said to be good for people who travel by land or sea, short or long journeys.

# TEA-CUP FORTUNE TELLING

There is no more interesting way of telling fortunes than by means of the leaves which are left in the dregs of a cup of tea. Let us describe the method. Suppose that a friend is sitting at your tea-table, and you propose to tell his or her fortune. The first thing is for the friend to drink the contents of the cup—this is absolutely necessary. There should be left about a teaspoonful of liquid in the cup. Place the saucer over the cup, swill the latter round for a moment and then drain out the liquid. Remove the saucer and examine the disposition of the tea-leaves. Sometimes, the leaves resolve themselves into very clear formations, when the rest becomes easy ; but at other times, it requires a careful scrutiny to recognise the shapes.

What the shapes stand for can be found by consulting the alphabetical list given in this chapter. Here it may be said that shapes arrayed close to the brim of the cup are likely to happen soon ; whilst those in the bottom of the cup may be long delayed ; that is unless the individual descriptions give any hint to the contrary.

ACORNS.—An acorn at the top of the cup foretells to the consultant riches easily gained.

In the middle, and in the clear, good health and enjoyment.

At the bottom of the cup, shows a certain recovery from a severe illness ; or if the consultant has financial difficulties to contend with, assistance is at hand and a way shown to surmount speedily all troubles.

ALPS.—High mountains with peaks are indicative of high aspirations and great endeavours, which will be successful if the attending symbols are propitious or the mountains appear in a clear field with lines across or bars or crosses around them. If these occur, then the ambitions will be realised only with great difficulty and not without danger.

AMULET.—A symbol of this sort of whatever nature, such as a heart, anchor, etc., should be interpreted according to the nature of the symbol ; but in general the amulet may be

48

said to indicate protection and good fortune, for that is the sole purpose of their existence and use.

ANCHOR.—At the bottom of the cup, success by water.

At the top, constant love.

In the middle, surrounded by dots, a voyage bringing success, good business and commerce, money by water.

Erect, with the link uppermost, well-deserved rest, with plenty.

Surrounded by thick clouds, inconstancy.

Dashes round about, dangerous enterprises, ultimate success.

ANKLE.—Joined to the upper leg, shows ability misdirected, ambition without understanding, and instability of purpose. Joined to a foot it indicates soundness of judgment, deep understanding, power of direction and control, and desire for progress. If turned to the right, it is an additional indication of good.

ANT.—This is a symbol of industry, courage, perseverance, and thrift. It shows success in life by the use of the natural powers and faculties and a place among the people as a well-known and deserving citizen.

ARROW.—This indicates a disagreeable letter; from where it comes must be judged by the direction of the arrow. If dots are around it will be connected with money.

ATTIRE.—Clothes of any sort are a symbol of a change of estate, for better or worse, as may be indicated by the nature of the article represented. A hat shows a rise in life, a new position, honours or preferment, success. Boots denote journeys, and if well defined will be successful. A habit or coat shows a change in your domestic affairs. A collar indicates a change of occupation.

BABY.—Curiously enough, this symbol is an indication of trouble and denotes the beginning of a new series of adversities which will claim much of your time and attention. If this symbol is attended by a star, do not sign any agreements or contracts and look well to those that are already standing, for they are in danger of collapse and nullity.

BAGPIPE.—There will be much discord and disaffection in your family affairs. Business will be conducted with difficulty. Excitement and high tension will tend to create ill-health and nervous derangement. Projects and ambitions end in discord and danger.

BAYONET.—Dangers beset you. Criticism and poignant enmity will tend to mar the otherwise placid condition of your

life. A thrust is made at you from one who is your rival. Your best powers are now required, and Truth, the two-edged sword of the victor, is your best weapon.

BEAR.—This brute of the lower creation of animals indicates that there is danger of running into danger through stupidity, and most probably meeting with obstacles that will call upon the brute force.

Irrational projects may land you far away from human sympathy.

BED.—This symbol is indicative of a state of mind which will produce direct results in your life and fortunes. If tidy and well-kept, then your fortunes will be good and your success in life assured. If disordered, it is a sign of trouble and want.

BEE.—This is one of the best of symbols, and when occurring, either by itself or in combination with other symbols, it denotes prosperity as the result of prudence and industry, the acquisition of fortune, amassing of wealth through international trade and purveying of all sorts of domestic and social happiness and success. It denotes good news, and to the needy it promises an entire change of fortune for good, and the access to much that is now only a dream.

BELL.—Observe the symbols attending this carefully, for it may be that it is a knell or a carillon of joy. The bell itself indicates an announcement which will be more or less widespread and will affect your fortunes very distinctly.

BOOT.—This denotes a protection from danger if well-defined and clear, but ill-formed or tattered it shows disgrace and loss of position and credit.

If the toe of the boot is pointing away from the handle, a speedy removal, the kick-out.

If at the top of the cup, a desire to travel.

If in the middle it advises caution as to the next movements.

If a circle is near it indicates a satisfactory completion.

BOTTLE.—Take warning from this symbol that you may need the help of a physician and observe the rules of health ; moderation in all things. Upright, there will be prolonged danger to the health and position ; but if reversed the symbol shows a speedy recovery in health and fortunes.

BRACELET.—The ring or bracelet is a sign of impending marriage or union of fortunes with another. It may be a bond of slavery and misfortune or of renewed strength and freedom, according to the attendant symbols. Of itself it is merely a badge of union and cannot be fully interpreted alone.

BRANCH.—A sprig or branch with leaves is a sign of a birth in the family within your own circle of relations. If without leaves it denotes sorrow and trouble, disappointed hopes, and barren ambitions.

BREAD.—Bread denotes sorrow and sickness, equally as happiness and health. Close attention must be paid to the surroundings and contiguous symbols. Your daily bread may be in jeopardy. Pray that it be sure. Give, but do not squander or waste.

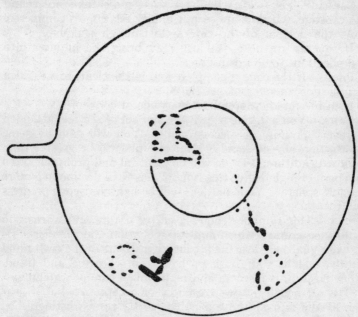

Tea-leaves depicting a boot, a roadway, a circle, the letter F, and a ring

BRIDE.—A figure dressed like a bride is a symbol of sorrow, the distinguishing feature being the veil. This indicates complications and perplexities coming in swarms, with consequent trouble and distress of mind.

BRIDGE.—This symbol denotes that you will be saved out of your troubles by most fortunate and kind intervention; that you will surmount your difficulties and make progress even in the face of obstacles. Your path is prepared—you have only to go forward in faith.

BUTTERFLY.—The butterfly indicates frivolity and innocent pleasure.

In the middle of the cup, beware of rushing into too much gaiety.

At the top of the cup, the butterfly indicates pleasures, and the consultant can, by being sincere and natural, become a very useful member of society.

Surrounded by dots, indiscreet extravagance and trouble in consequence.

CABBAGE.—Notice particularly what indications are round the cabbage. If dots are seen, jealousy relating to commerce.

At the bottom of the cup, spite through jealousy.

If squares are near, jealousy may bring the inquirer into complications, or even disgrace.

CAGE.—If the cage is complete and in the clear, to a maiden it indicates an offer of marriage.

If in the middle, foretells a marriage of convenience.

CART.—You are here shown the symbol of service, attended by every promise of success in life. You will gain by some transaction now in hand. Your receipts will be greater than your expenditure. Trade will be plentiful and profitable. To one born of high degree this symbol denotes a decline to a more humble sphere. Your burdens will be light and your progress swift.

CAT.—This symbol denotes a crafty nature and warns you of lurking enmity which aims at spoliation and plunder. Be on your guard against the predatory instincts of the crafty and subtle, and in your business beware of cheating and fraud. Your position is insecure and needs much careful watching.

The cat usually shows treachery or deception ; but if near the handle and at the top of the cup a cat is distinguished in a resting position, it shows domestic comfort.

CHURCH.—This is a sign of ceremonial. Some formalities will be observed in relation to a marriage, birth, or death, according to the attendant indications or adjacent symbols. Your work will lie in association with others of like ambitions and views. If the spire be clear and well-defined you will succeed.

CIGAR.—Be careful that your best projects do not end in smoke. You have dreams of independence and luxury. It is doubtful whether you will realise them. Thrift, economy, and steadfastness will be needed to bring you through.

CIRCLE.—This is the perfect form, and by compliance with the natural order of things and the observance of duty in all

respects you will achieve your end and bring your work to perfection.

COFFIN.—The semblance of a coffin does not always foretell a death. Usually it means a tedious illness, and shows that great care should be taken.

It also denotes a probable failure in business.

COIN.—A sign of gain and prosperity, and of obligations which will arise in connection with your business affairs. If well-defined, you will meet your liabilities, but if broken on the rim it denotes failure and need for financial help.

COLLAR.—A sign of servitude and dependence. Your success will lie with others, and by your associations you will succeed or fail in life. Be careful in the choice of your friends and advisers. Hitch your wagon to a star. Your greatness will depend on your powers of service to another or others. Fidelity and industry are your great assets.

CROSS.—A symbol of suffering and application to duty in the face of great temptations and difficulties. You will be asked to make some sacrifice for the good of those beloved by you, and will do it. Your present projects will show losses and disappointments. You will have much need for courage and faith.

The cross is always suggestive of suffering.

In the clear it is indicative of troubles that can be overcome by perseverance and faith.

At the top of the cup, delayed desires.

At the bottom, great trials.

Two crosses, severe affliction.

CROWN.—The symbol of supremacy, denoting ascendancy over all difficulties and elevation to positions of high degree, with increase of power and influence. What you have in hand will lead to success. Some will achieve greatness and others have greatness thrust upon them. In all cases there is success but with increased responsibility.

If straight lines are close to it the crown signifies a straight course to honours.

If wavy lines are around, there will be delays and obstacles in the way of deserved honours.

DAGGER.—The short sword is a symbol of strife and enmity. Appearing with other symbols it is a menace of the gravest nature, and in all cases a sign of great need for watchfulness in all things.

Beware of being too hasty in any undertaking on hand.

DAISY.—This emblem of simplicity would suggest happiness in the spring, or, if it should take the form of the more stately Marguerite, the debutante will have a joyous and successful season. Many admirers.

DOG.—This symbol is always an indication of friendship and fidelity. It indicates that in all circumstances and upon all occasions you can rely upon the advice and assistance of your

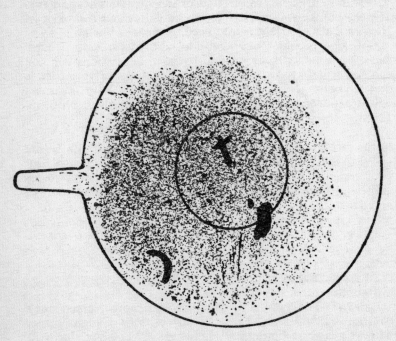

Tea-leaves depicting a cross, a moon and a satellite

friends. If recumbent or lying down, the dog shows safety and peace around you ; but if barking or active, there will be occasion for the activity of your friends.

The dog is always an emblem of fidelity and shows true friends. However, the position even of this faithful creature has a twofold meaning.

If his image is surrounded with dashes and clouds it shows that your friends are estranged from you through the envy of someone unworthy of your confidence.

If at the bottom of the cup, a friend is in trouble.

A dog appearing to be running or capering indicates joyful news and a meeting of dear friends.

DUMB-BELL.—This symbol denotes stress and strife. It is a sign of hard work and little profit, with continual rivalry and opposition. This being your experience, make a change of occupation and surroundings and so relieve the pressure upon you.

EAGLE.—This symbol is very fortunate and indicates aspirations which will meet with the highest success. In the world of ideas, whether industrial, political, or commercial, or even in social life, there will be assured recognition. You will attain to a much higher position than that of your birth, and this by the right use of your powers.

EGG.—This is always a symbol of beneficial changes and new projects. Success attends your efforts in all directions if the appearance is symmetrical and well-defined, but if broken you may expect failure in some new undertaking. To the married it frequently portends an addition to the family.

EYE.—The symbol of intelligence and the fruits of well-applied faculty. It denotes mental and spiritual discernment and more than ordinary power of foresight.

To see this organ of sight in the cup advises inquirers to be careful in their business dealings and to inspect carefully any proposition put before them.

FAN.—This is a symbol of false friends and scandal from which you are liable to suffer hurt.

A fan in the clear at the top of the cup denotes innocent flirtations.

Near the handle, an invitation to a place of amusement. With wavy lines, indiscretion, coquetry.

In the thick, vexation, pique.

FEATHER.—The sign of inconstancy and levity. You are warned to take a more serious view of your actions and deportment. Relaxation and pleasure should follow steadfast work and earnest endeavour and not be made the business of life.

FERN.—This symbol denotes inconstancy in your affections. You will have domestic trouble and social scandal.

It is said that a man should never give his sweetheart ferns. Perhaps that is why the interpretation here is that there is restlessness in the air, a change of desires and places.

FISH.—There are few symbols more fortunate than this. It denotes great increase and prosperity in all affairs, affluence and a multiplicity of profitable interests.

A fish is always a lucky emblem. If surrounded with dots it denotes wealth acquired through a lucky speculation.

If wavy lines are near, it denotes that the fortunes fluctuate.

Take particular notice of any emblems near to the fish and look upon them as a guide to becoming a successful financier.

GALLOWS.—The gallows denotes extreme danger of financial or social failure. You are warned to measure the cost of your every action and to avoid impulse.

GRAPES.—The symbol of grapes is very fortunate and shows increase and prosperity, but yet much burden to carry through life, but power to get, to have, and to hold.

Grapes denote ambitions in love gratified in all seasons.

HAMMER.—This symbol denotes stress and emphasis. It indicates need for continual and unremitting employment of the faculties and constant reiteration of desires, in order that your ambitions may be realised. Persistence is your watchword.

HAND.—If well-defined this symbol denotes friendship, assistance, good works, and success ; but if cramped, folded, imperfect, or ill-formed, it is a symbol of failure to achieve your ambitions through lack of natural faculty or application of your powers.

HAT.—This is a symbol of a new occupation, fresh projects, and new ambitions. You will meet with preferment and your position will soon improve. To a woman it denotes marriage, or at least a higher estate.

At the bottom of the cup, a rival. In the clear, honours.

HEART.—This symbol indicates a genuine and trustworthy person whose affections will be well-placed and whose life will abound in good works and happy associations. To the young it shows engagement in marriage, and to those of more advanced years marriage or a very close friendship.

If a crown should be near a heart it denotes honours. If dots are near, financial gain and true love.

A fruit near, pleasures.

Two hearts together, certain marriage. If a letter can be seen near, it signifies the initial of the person's name.

HIVE.—A hive is a symbol of a home. If there is a swarm of bees it is a sign of the highest success in some industrial or social field of activity. You may depend on the reward of your labours.

HORSESHOE.—This is universally a symbol of good fortune by some hazard or lucky incident. If near the handle of cup it will be very soon realised.

HOUR-GLASS.—This symbol denotes that what you have to do must be done quickly, for the time of the reaping is nigh. Time and tide wait for no man.

If this symbol is seen anywhere in the cup it warns you to be watchful over those dear to you. To be circumspect in your business and in your domestic life.

In the thick, imminent danger and peril.

At the bottom, danger in the future through present neglect of duty.

HOUSE.—This symbol is an indication of possession and safety. It denotes a happy and prosperous life, which, however humble, will bring the sweet satisfaction of independence.

At the top of the cup, success in business. A good change of abode. If the present state of affairs is not favourable, this indicates a speedy change for the better. Great success in any new enterprises. Good for engaging new employees.

IVY.—A sign of loyal friends. Should you decipher this at the bottom of the cup, then prepare for sad news of a well-loved friend.

In the clear or at the top of the cup, there will be a gathering of true friends, or an invitation to a large house-party.

One ivy leaf in the clear, a devoted and faithful lover.

KETTLE.—A sign of domestic happiness and success through industry.

This symbol has a two fold meaning. If rightly placed, near the handle of the cup, and in the clear, it shows domestic efficiency and comfort with consequent happiness.

LADDER.—In the clear shows advancement. If dots are close to it, ambitions arrived at through money.

It is generally good to find the semblance of a ladder in the tea-cup, as it promises advancement through industry, and though gradual will be permanent.

If the ladder is not very distinct, others will interfere and delay your projects.

LADLE.—This symbol denotes good fortune and the timely aid of friends towards some project now in course of pursuance.

LEAVES.—Leaves show happiness and success. Should they be at the bottom of the cup they denote that success will come in later life.

LEG.—This symbol is a sign of strength and fortitude. It denotes progress and advancement in life, and if attached to

the foot denotes unusual sagacity and understanding of men and things.

LOOP.—This symbol denotes a danger of entanglement, and is really in the nature of a snare or trap of which you should be aware if you look well ahead.

MOON.—Surrounded by clouds it denotes depression and tears. A full moon in the clear suggests a romantic attachment, probably an elopement. If straight lines are near all will end happily ; but if wavy lines or a cross or a comet surrounds it, trouble will arise, and regret will follow.

The first quarter of the moon indicates new ideas, the opening of new projects. The last quarter warns you to refrain from taking up any new undertaking and to be wary of travelling by water.

MUSHROOM.—In the clear this foretells a change to a country home. Remember that the handle of the cup represents the north, so the direction of the home can be traced according to the position of the emblem. At the top of the cup it indicates sudden exaltation to honours and position.

If the right way up, at the bottom of the cup, it indicates rapidity of growth. Reversed, expect reversals, frustrated hopes, and unsettled business ; even loss of position.

Should the head of the mushroom be towards the handle, there is every possibility of saving the situation by great energy and foresight ; therefore, remember the saying : " Forewarned is to be forearmed." Look well into your business.

NAIL.—This symbol denotes malice and cruelty which may be directed against you. Your feelings are going to be severely wounded.

If at the top, a sudden and sharp affliction. Frequently an injury or great injustice will be inflicted on the unwary.

OATS.—This is a symbol of a stalwart and genuine character, who is capable of rising in life through industry and disregard of frivolity and pleasures. A plain, humble, and steadfast nature. It denotes good prospects and the sure reward of industry and thrift.

PIGS.—The pig indicates a mixture of good and bad luck. It generally denotes good luck, but there is danger of excess and self-indulgence.

PILLAR.—The symbol of strength and steadfastness. You will inspire confidence in others, and they will depend on your

ability and strength. Your position will become established and much responsibility will rest on you.

PINCERS.—The symbol of stress and difficulty. You are faced with some hard problem which will require all your ability to negotiate. Be careful that you do not get into the grip of necessity or the law.

PYRAMID.—This is a symbol of a great revelation—a secret held that will finally be discovered. You may be the victim

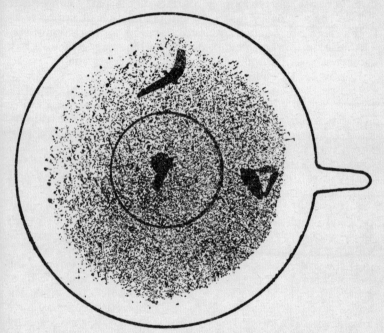

Tea-leaves depicting a revolver, a pyramid, and a rudder

of some family secret or complex circumstance which has held you back, but which now will be solved to your satisfaction and great benefit. It is a sign of coming good fortune.

REVOLVER.—The pistol, gun, or revolver denotes a sharp decision which arises out of dispute or enmity. You will be called upon shortly to take some decisive step or to engage in a contest of powers in which your future interests are very largely involved.

RING.—This is always a sign of amity and goodwill, and usually is followed by events of importance in life. It denotes

a completion of projects, success, eventuality, a new order of things, fresh circumstances, lasting good. To the young this symbol foretells speedy marriage, especially if associated with flowers, the heart symbol, or the cup. With the anchor it denotes engagement.

The ring is a sign of marriage if quite clear and near the top. When the ring is in the middle of the cup and is not quite smooth all round it denotes an offer of marriage. A letter near in either case will denote the initials of the party concerned.

Two rings, a hasty marriage and completion of projects.

If a ring is surrounded by clouds it will be wise to be cautious.

At the bottom of the cup, denotes a long engagement ; but should a cross be quite near, a broken engagement.

ROADWAY.—Denotes a journey.

RUDDER.—This symbol denotes providential guidance in the conduct of your affairs. You may be the means of guiding others to safety and rest. You have special faculty for training and teaching. At present there are signs of important decisions and a turn in affairs generally.

SATELLITE.—A large body with a smaller one near it shows that you will be subservient most of your days to someone of higher position and greater power.

SCALES.—If the scales are evenly balanced the augury must be good ; but should either side be weighed down it would show wrong judgment, even an unbalanced mind—certainly failure and want of foresight.

If the scales are at the bottom of the cup, a lawsuit, and the case will surely go against you. If in the clear, and you have a lawsuit on hand, success. It would also denote completion and a very satisfactory reply to any proposition you may have advanced. If a sword should be near the scales, then a speedy judgment will be meted out.

SCEPTRE.—The symbol of authority and command. Your fortunes are assured and your position in life will be unassailable. But be careful how you use your influence. In any issue now impending you will be the victor.

The sceptre, an emblem of power and authority, seen in the clear denotes that the consultant will receive an honour from royalty.

Near the house—i.e. the handle—signifies that the consultant will be offered a position of authority.

At the bottom of the cup, honours and work appreciated later in life.

SCISSORS.—Denotes cross-purposes, misunderstandings, and bickering. Defer to the opinions of others in matters of doubt. Do not cut hay in a hurricane.

At the top of the cup, separation. In the clear, the end of a quarrel.

At the bottom of the cup and in the thick, quarrels and disturbances.

At the handle, unrest in the home.

SHIP.—A symbol of fortune if in full sail, well-defined and clear. If the sails or rigging are tattered you are in danger of wreck or ruin. If proceeding to the left it is a further sign of disaster. Of a roaming and inconsequent nature, you have need of a guiding star. You may find such in a friend or a partner. Hitch up and follow it.

SLIPPER.—You are quite unsuited for the sterner work of the world, and, as a person given to considerable self-indulgence, you will find a soft corner somewhere where you are wanted. You will have more good fortune than comes to most people in your sphere of life. You can bring comfort where strength is unavailing. You will play your part in advanced years.

SLUG.—A symbol of parasitic and indolent nature. There is need at present for some action which seems entirely beyond your powers. Nevertheless, attempt it. The easy path of self-indulgence leads nowhere worth while.

SNAKE.—This indicates inveterate enemies.

On the top or middle of the cup, if clear, it promises triumph over an enemy, but not easily obtained if the snake is in the thick, or cloudy.

If a letter appears near the emblem it will be easy to discover the name of the enemy. If near the handle it shows there is someone in the house who is unworthy of trust.

STAR.—A star formed by the crossing of three lines is fortunate and denotes some coming good fortune and splendid opportunity for advancement in life. But if formed of four lines crossing, it is of evil import and warns of sudden dangers, accidents, and catastrophes.

At the top, love and honour. If dots are about it, it foretells great fortune, wealth, high respectability, honours. Several stars denote good and happy children. A star surrounded by dashes and in the thick, a warning that good fortune is weakening. Look well to your home affairs and business. Clouded shows long life though many troubles.

STATUE.—A mark of distinction. You have power to make

your name famous in the annals of your time; but if you have no more heart than a statue of stone, you will need to reform yourself before reforming the world. Just now you have honours and invitations which your position does not allow you to accept. Break through your limitations and court success.

STEEPLE.—The spire or steeple is an indication of an ambitious and yet lofty nature, capable of earning distinction

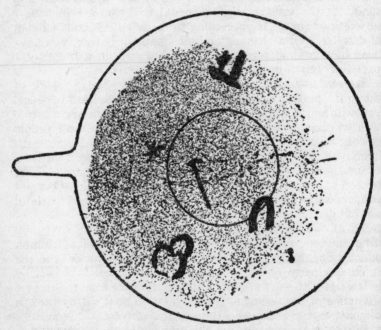

Tea-leaves depicting a star, a horseshoe, a nail, a gibbet, and bread

and standing as an example of lofty aspirations to others. You live at present in hope of preferment. You will get it. Your ambitions will be realised.

TREE.—Several trees, your wishes will be gratified.

A single tree, lasting good health, and position.

An oak tree, riches and comfort; protection.

A tree surrounded by dots, your fortune in the country.

TRIANGLE.—Always a fortunate figure when intact and well-defined.

Triangles are a sign of good and bad luck according to the position of the triangle.

With the apex uppermost—i.e. nearest the rim of cup—it is a sign of good fortune and success, of new and successful enterprises, ambitions, achieved hopes realised.

With the base uppermost its indication is sinister and indicative of loss and failure in all immediate enterprises and projects. It warns you of dangers arising from giving a too free rein to your passions and desires, and cautions you to observe moderation in all things. In the strife between brain and heart, reason and impulse, you will fail if you do not follow the dictates of reason.

If the apex of the triangle is uppermost and pointing due north—i.e. the handle of the cup—you will have material gain. If south, honours and preferment. If west, a beneficial alliance or partnership, and if the inquirer is a maiden, marriage. While if the apex is towards the east, new avenues will be opened up before you, with fresh projects and enterprises which will prove highly successful.

VESSEL.—Vessels of all kinds are containers, and according to their several proportions, lineaments, and uses must be regarded as indicating a measure of inherent capacity for service. Most frequently they indicate people of great natural ability and resourcefulness, sometimes the very learned or capable, but rather reclusive and undemonstrative, careful and often selfish. A vessel denotes the reception of some benefit which is the expression of a person's affection.

WHEEL.—A wheel at the top of the cup indicates that an inheritance is about to fall to the consultant.

If engaged in mechanical work it shows progress by the use of your faculty. To all others it denotes a stern necessity, a life subject to time and circumstance. As " Sepharial " says : " We cannot evade the inevitable, but we can make use of it."

# WILL MY WISH COME TRUE ?

Have you something on your mind that you are wondering whether it will come true or not ? If so, consult this lucky oracle. Note that it is no use framing a question, just to see how the answer comes. The question must be one that you have long pondered over.

First, open the book flat, so that the page is perfectly level : then take out the four queens from a pack of cards and place the Queen of Hearts on the top edge of the picture, the Queen of Clubs on the bottom edge, the Queen of Diamonds on the left-hand side, and the Queen of Spades on the right-hand side.

All being ready, think of the question, repeating it to yourself, under your breath : then spin a coin on the picture. Wait for it to come to rest. If it falls so as to touch any of the circles containing the head of a king, your wish will come true. In the event of the coin falling entirely within one of the circles, the wish will be granted quite soon. We do not say that the wish will be refused, if the coin falls entirely on the shaded part, but it is not likely to be granted, at least for a long time.

If the coin runs off the picture, try again.

This lucky wish method will also interest your friends at a party gathering.

Will My Wish come True ?

# WHAT DO THE DICE PREDICT ?

Now, let us see what dice can tell us of our luck. Take three dice, shake them well in the box with your left hand, and then cast them out on a table, on which you have previously drawn a circle with chalk, but never throw on a Monday or Wednesday. The total value of the three dice as thrown should be interpreted as follows :—

THREE.—A pleasing surprise.

FOUR.—A disagreeable one.

FIVE.—A stranger, who will prove a friend.

SIX.—Loss of property.

SEVEN.—Undeserved scandal.

EIGHT.—Merited reproach.

NINE.—A wedding.

TEN.—A christening, at which some important event will occur to you.

ELEVEN.—A death that concerns you.

TWELVE.—A letter, speedily.

THIRTEEN.—Tears and sighs.

FOURTEEN.—A new admirer.

FIFTEEN.—Beware that you are not drawn into some trouble or plot.

SIXTEEN.—A pleasant journey.

SEVENTEEN.—You will either be on the water, or have dealings with those belonging to it, to your advantage.

EIGHTEEN.—A great profit, rise in life, or some desirable good will happen immediately ; for answers to dice are always fulfilled within nine days.

To show the same number twice at one trial, shows news from abroad, whatever be the number. If the dice roll over the circle, the number thrown goes for nothing, but it shows sharp words, and if they fall to the floor, it is blows ; in throwing out the dice, if one remains on the top of the other, it is a present, of which females must take care.

# DOMINOES TELL YOUR FORTUNE

Take a set of dominoes, shuffle well while the faces are downwards : then, with the left hand, pick one at random. This is what each domino means :

DOUBLE-SIX.—Receiving a handsome sum of money.

SIX-FIVE.—Going to a public amusement.

SIX-FOUR.—Law-suits.

SIX-THREE.—Ride in a car.

SIX-TWO.—Present of clothing.

SIX-ONE.—You will soon perform a friendly action.

SIX-BLANK.—Guard against scandal, or you will suffer by your inattention.

DOUBLE-FIVE.—A new abode to your advantage.

FIVE-FOUR.—A fortunate speculation.

FIVE-THREE.—A visit from a superior.

FIVE-TWO.—A water party.

FIVE-ONE.—A love intrigue.

FIVE-BLANK.—A funeral, but not of a relation.

DOUBLE-FOUR.—Drinking liquor at a distance.

FOUR-THREE.—A false alarm at your house.

FOUR-TWO.—Beware of thieves or swindlers. Ladies, notice this ; it means more than it says.

FOUR-ONE.—Trouble from creditors.

FOUR-BLANK.—A letter from an angry friend.

DOUBLE-THREE.—Sudden wedding, at which you will be vexed.

THREE-TWO.—Buy no lottery tickets, nor enter into any game of chance, or you will lose.

THREE-ONE.—A great discovery at hand.

THREE-BLANK.—An illegitimate child.

DOUBLE-TWO.—Plagued by a jealous partner.

TWO-ONE.—You will mortgage or pledge some property very soon.

DOUBLE-ONE.—You will soon find something to your advantage in the street or road.

DOUBLE-BLANK.—The worst presage in all the set of dominoes : you will live a life that will be colourless.

You should never draw more than two dominoes during the same moon. The two readings may be averaged together, a good omen lessening the effect of one that is bad, and vice-versa. More than two draws will only deceive you.

# THE MOTOR ORACLE

    Shut your eyes and pick out any letter with a pin or pencil point. At the same time, hold a map in your left hand. Some piece of great good fortune will come to you while riding in a motor car, or other vehicle, having the chosen letter as one of its index letters.

# FORTUNE TELLING
# ON
# HALLOWE'EN

On the evening of October 31st, each year, the spirits of divination are supposed to be particularly active and at no other time is it so propitious to ask favours of them. Thus it comes about that youths and maidens have, from time immemorial, practised certain rituals on Hallowe'en. For the sake of those who do not know the regular fortune-telling games, associated with this occasion, they are set out here.

## Burning The Nuts

A favourite method of consulting the future, because it was certain to reveal the truth, was to throw two nuts into the fire. If they burnt brightly, then a happy marriage was certain. If one nut burnt steadily, while the other popped and spluttered, then quarrels were probable, with a possibility of " making-up " the differences afterwards. But, if both nuts proved sulky, then trouble could certainly be expected.

## The Apple Peel

Another very simple, yet very truthful, way of seeking information from the Fates was for a maiden to peel an apple. It had to be done entirely in one strip. Then, the peel was carefully tossed over the left shoulder by means of the right hand. As the peel lay on the floor, it was examined to see if it assumed the shape of a letter. That letter gave the initial of the maiden's lover.

## The Ash Sprig

A party of young people of both sexes go out into a wood and search among the ash trees. What they seek to find is " an even-leaved sprig." The first man and the first maid to find such a treasure are bound to become sweethearts.

# The Three Dishes

Probably, this method of fortune-telling is the greatest favourite of all. Three dishes are taken : one is filled with clean water, another with dirty water, and a third is left empty. These are placed side by side on a table, while the young people are facing the other way. Then, in turn, man and maid is blindfolded and led to the table, the position of the dishes being changed each time.

The players poke the ring-finger into any dish they like and the Fates duly oblige with an answer. The clean water shows a happy marriage, the dirty water a troublesome and stormy union, while the empty bowl shows that no marriage in probable until the next Hallowe'en comes along.

# The Apple Charm

A maid retires into a darkened room, all alone and without letting anyone know of her actions. She holds a lighted candle in her hand and approaches a mirror : she peers into the mirror and eats an apple, or she combs her hair—whichever she pleases.

While she is doing this, her imaginations are allowed full play and, if she is lucky, she spies the features of a young man in the glass, looking over her shoulders. This young man is her future husband.

# The Wet Shirt Sleeve

Many a country girl anxious to see the face of her future husband would wet a shirt-sleeve and hang it before the fire to dry, then lie in bed watching it till midnight. When that magical hour approached the apparition of her future life's partner would appear and turn the sleeve. She must on no account speak or make any movement but lie with her eyes fixed on him until he turned to face her. The moment he did so she must start to count quietly in her own mind and the number she reached before he disappeared would be the number of years they would live together happily.

# The Lighted Candles

It is usual to set two lighted candles over the fireplace and, from the way they burn, so you can tell the luck of the whole household, during the coming year.

If they are consumed brightly, then there is good fortune for all the family : if they smoke and splutter, reverses will have to be met : and if they just burn in an ordinary way, then the luck will be ordinary.

# The Bowl of Fire

Not the least amusing game of fortunes is provided by a large bowl of water, set on the hearth in front of a bright fire. The flames and the glowing embers will mirror themselves in the water, if the bowl is set in the right place.

Just watch the surface and be very careful not to look at the fire, for such is highly unlucky. What shapes and images are revealed in the water ! The first that each person can discern is a message to him or her. It has a particular meaning. What the meaning is can be recognised by looking through the chapter which interprets the shapes found in teacups. For the meanings of the things seen on the surface of the bowl are exactly the same as if formed by tea leaves.

# YOUR
# LUCKY MONTH

## THE WHEEL OF LUCK

Would you like to know which is going to be your luckiest month in the coming year? Here is a device which will tell you in a few moments. Two illustrations are given: both have to be cut out; the one, known as the four queens, being placed centrally over the circle of months. Run a pin through both centres, in such a way that the two circles can revolve, one over the other. (See pages 73 and 75.)

Now what you have to do is this: with your eyes shut, turn the two wheels or discs as much or little as you like. Then open your eyes and see where they have come to rest.

Note that on the wheel of four queens, there is a white outer band, bearing the four card signs. If the day of the month on which you are consulting your Fates is

(*a*) From the first to the seventh, then observe the arrow indicated by the heart and ignore the other three.

(*b*) From the eighth to the fifteenth, then observe the arrow indicated by the spade.

(*c*) From the sixteenth to the twenty-third, then observe the arrow indicated by the club.

(*d*) From the twenty-fourth to the thirty-first, then observe the arrow indicated by the diamond.

Your arrow will point to a section, marked with a month, on the larger wheel. The month, so indicated, is the one which the Fates have singled out to be a very lucky one for you.

This consultation of the Fates may be attempted at any time of the year. The answer applies to the twelve months that are going to follow, commencing on the first day of the next month. It should be remembered that only one attempt in any year is recognised by the Fates, all others are merely ignored.

THE WHEEL OF LUCK

THE WHEEL OF LUCK

# CHARACTER AND HANDWRITING

Handwriting is a sure guide to character. Therefore, take that letter which you received from your friend and we will tell you all about him or her.

Spread out the letter and select any word, at random, which commences with a capital—the longer the word the better, because it gives you more to work upon.

First.—Rule a horizontal line, immediately below the word and parallel to the top edge of the paper. If the word keeps in line with the ruled mark, the friend is a level-headed person, probably of even temper. Should the word run up away from the line, he possesses character and there are many things he can do better than the average person can. If, however, the word runs down and cuts through the line, he is one who misses chances.

2nd.—Are the downstrokes of the letters considerably thicker than the upstrokes? If so, his is a nature that worries over trifles.

3rd.—Is the capital disjointed from the rest of the word? If it is, he is easy-going, large-minded and, probably, over charitable. Should the whole word be in one piece, he is eminently practical. If all the letters are separate, it shows that he likes to take life easily, though it may be that he has a strain of the " artistic " in his nature.

4th.—If the loops of the letters are turned into points, he is practical and broad-minded.

5th.—Are the letters rounded? Then he is affable and has a full share of affection.

6th.—Is every letter properly formed? For instance, should there be an *e*, is it given its loop or is it blind; does the *a* close up as it should; has the *c* its requisite dot, and so on? If you can say " yes " to all these questions, he is methodical and has a tidy nature.

7th.—Do the loops joining such letters as an *a* and an *r*, and an *a* and a *c* come down to the line, or do they join up

John Keats    T. Campbell

Byron

Thos. De Quincy    C Lamb

Thos. Hood

H.W. Longfellow

Macaulay    Wm Thackeray.

Robert Browning.    P B Shelly

George Eliot    John Dryden..

T. Carlyl    John Milton.

John Bunyon

close to the top of the letters?    His judgment is sound if
the former is the case, but far less so, if the latter.

8th.—Is the slope of the whole word, from right to left,
backhanded, as it is sometimes called?    Should it lean in this
direction, he has a feeling for artistic things.

9th.—Is the general effect of the word " curly," and are there several flourishes ? He is a comfortable kind of person, —one that makes others quickly feel at home.

10th.—Is the bottom half of the word much blacker with ink than the top half ? Should it be, he has a scientific mind and might be an inventor.

11th.—Did he dash a line under his signature, by way of a finish ? People with inferiority complexes never do that. If he supplied such a line, it is safe to claim that he is well-pleased with himself.

So much for the analysis of the test word : now, perhaps, you would like to go a little deeper into this fascinating subject. The best thing to do under these circumstances would be to take a page of his ordinary handwriting, and to let us analyse it together.

First of all, is it big writing, nigglingly small writing, or of just ordinary size ? It is quite easy to tell the writer's nature by applying this simple test, and it is a test that seldom goes wrong. Big writing shows a big mind, a kind heart and a generous person. Nigglingly small writing betrays the narrow mind of a person who is not by any means generous. Writing of ordinary size is the work of the average person, someone who is not outstanding in either merit or defective qualities.

Now for the slope of the letters. It has already been said that backhanded writing reveals an artistic mind. There is, also, the style of writing to consider that is very much upright, as well as very much slanting to the right. The first shows a nature that is very determined. It belongs to a person who knows exactly what he wants and he sees that he gets it. Mind, there is no discredit to be attached to him : he is merely very efficient. The other kind of writing, that in which there is an abnormal amount of slope to the right, reveals a person who *enjoys* looking on the gloomy side of life, and the more the slope the deeper the gloom.

The next test concerns only the capitals. Do you find that the writer has a weakness for printing them, rather than writing them ? Many people have this habit and, as a rule, they are people who are fond of criticising. They are never likely to lose an opportunity of pulling somebody to bits, and they do not always do it nicely, either.

Capitals can reveal another insight into character. Certain of them have been modernised in shape, during the last fifty years. The A, for instance, used to possess a large curl

Here are three types of Handwriting. All show an educated mind : otherwise they are very different. Their characteristic features are dealt with in this chapter.

wrapped round its middle. The B was done in two separate parts, one of which was something like the figure 3, and so on. Now, if a person adheres to these old forms it is conclusive proof that he is old-fashioned in his ideas. More than likely, he is the type of person who is loud in denouncing the youth of to-day.

Now let us take a few letters separately. In a page of writing, the letter *t* is sure to come frequently. Has it been crossed with an inordinately long line, as long perhaps as the whole word. If so, the writer is a person of strong likes and dislikes. Moreover, he is a little " slap-dash."

Has he crossed the *t* very low down, so that far more of the upright is above the crossing than below it ? If he does this, it would be a mistake to leave a baby or a kitten in his care. He lacks kindness.

Has he formed the *t* in the old-fashioned way, with a curl across the middle of the upright ? He is secretive and deep, if he has.

Let us turn to the small *a*. Is the enclosed part not oval, but spiral ? This is a sign that the writer, though usually prim and proper, enjoys an occasional outburst of hilarity.

Does he make a small *e* something like a reversed 3 ? If this is so, it is a sign that he is not only efficient, but that he is very well pleased with himself.

Do you find that when an *m* or *n* comes at the end of a word, the writer makes practically no length of upward curl ? It is a sign of an egoistic nature. The person does not give away much. On the other hand, if there is a good length of curl or flourish as a finish to these letters, he is generous.

Does the writer make the small *g* like a *q* by looping the downward part the wrong way round ? This little habit reveals him as an individual who does not intend to bother overmuch about details.

Now, we will set out a number of personal characteristics and give the kind of writing that is associated with them.

## Physical Characteristics

*Activity.*—Persons of a particularly active disposition usually write a fairly regular hand, medium to moderately thick letters, strokes inclined to be upright, and a dash of movement about the signature, with perhaps a tendency just apparent for it to rise along its length.

*Ambition.*—An invariable sign of this is the constant rise in the whole of the writing.

*Calmness* is generally marked by clear writing and a uniformity in the shape of the letters, which are open and round. Capitals are small and well-made, and the line of the writing is even and firm.

*Courage.*—This is usually associated with the signs of an ambitious temperament ; a rising slope to the lines across the page. Also, there is a " dash " about the way the letters are formed.

*Enthusiasm* is a composite characteristic, and we may expect to find it in those who exhibit warmness of disposition, with energy and ambition. The enthusiastic person generally writes with a dash and fire, with ascending lines and flowing, easy capitals. All the *t*'s are well-barred, and there is some irregularity in the formation of the letters.

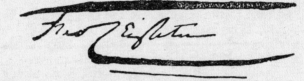

There is art and boldness in this Signature. The different heights of the letters suggest a strong imagination.

*Energy* is usually distinguished in handwriting by angles rather than rounded curves, ascendant lines, with a low-barred *t* and very definitely defined downstrokes. Energy may be combined with ambition or not. It may be seen with or without imagination or intuition. It amplifies the possession of either of these qualities if present with them.

*Indolence,* as might be expected, gives the reverse impressions to the above. There is an absence of angles or decision in the strokes, which are represented by rather rounded, spineless and languid curves. The handwriting, in fact, suggests a writer who is too lazy to form the letters. This is particularly apparent towards the end of a word where the tendency is to develop into a scrawl. The difference between this and the writing of the impatient person is evident. In the latter case the writing is angular and impetuous in form.

*Impulse* is seen in a handwriting in which freedom of movement, angularity in form, and large capitals predominate. Downstrokes and upstrokes in *h* and *g* and *l* and *y*, for example, show this tendency to elongation, and rapidity of movement is betrayed by a slope and continuous joinings of the letters and words.

*Obstinacy* will be revealed by clear, readable writing which is not picturesque to look at. There will be a certain amount

of labour in the formation of the letters and the writing will curve up, and, then, return to the original level. In a word, the handwriting is babyish.

*Perseverance* is a quality which is a compound of, or at least usually found in combination with, energy, patience and will. The writing is usually angular rather than rounded, with straight and rigid lines across the page. Frequently, there is an absence of imagination or originality—the capitals are, therefore, undistinguished in size or form. The *t* is well-barred, punctuation is well-marked, and the finals carried well forward, but low down.

## Intellectual Qualities

*Caution.*—This is marked in a handwriting which often shows many other qualities also. It is rarely found as a predominant trait. Caution may be observed in a precision of detail in the writing. Most careful punctuation, usually a dash instead of, or in addition to, the normal stops. The writing is usually upright and compressed. Generally it shows little trace of imagination. Often it has the marks of intuition.

This Signature shows that the individual has imaginative power, will-power and artistic perception.

*Imagination* is often shown in the size and shape of the capitals—large and original in form. The handwriting as a whole often becomes nearly illegible owing to the rapidity of its execution in striving to keep pace with the thought of the writer. The letters are generally irregular in size—the most usual form is the tendency to angularity, but the writing of the imaginative individual is sometimes rounded, denoting tenderness.

*Intuition* is generally marked by letters which are disjointed in the signature. The angular form of letter is the usual in which intuition is most marked, as this form is indicative of energy and impulsiveness. Both these qualities are allied to

the rapidity of thought processes associated with intuition. But whereas the former two qualities may be normally suggestive of rapidity, without a laboured judgment and possibly therefore misdirection, on the other hand intuition suggests quick penetrative and analytical capacity and correct judgment. In the one case the letters are connected—in the other, intuition, they are disconnected.

*Judgment.*—When this is the result of deduction, a sequence of thought processes logically followed out, from the general to the particular, it is generally marked by a handwriting in which not only the letters, but even words themselves, are joined in a complete sequence. There are flourishes and meaningless additions which help to make every page of the writing a pattern of curls and flourishes.

*Originality* is usually displayed in the shapes of the capital letters, and indeed of the others also. It is as though the power of the mind controlled, as no doubt it does, the hand wielding the pen. There is no conscious striving after eccentricity of form. The latter is rather indicative of vanity. The person with marked originality forms his letters as he does because this best expresses his revolt against convention.

*Sensitiveness* may be of two different kinds. It may be the response to artistic feeling, or more nearly a moral characteristic, a sympathetic feeling for others. In both cases, it is marked by a tendency to slope and curve in the letters. There is an absence of angularity and stiffness, and no self-assertiveness, upright characters or hardness in line and stroke, appears. The writing, like the character of the person, is softer, rounder, and more respondent to outside influences.

A Signature showing, above all, a versatile nature.

*Versatility*, like imagination, is marked by a difference in the height of the letters and by the peculiar forms of the letters, which tend to become spear-shaped in the loops. In the signature of Lytton Bulwer, a most versatile mind, it will be seen, too, that the characters are well-formed, and not, as with the purely imaginative person, becoming illegible.

*Will.*—Perhaps the best indication is that of the bar-like crossing of the *t*, and possibly a short bar beneath the signature. The downstrokes are firm, and descending letters like *g* and *y* show this firm stroke very plainly. Will is generally associated with persons of energetic and self-assertive temperament, and the handwriting is, therefore, frequently of the angular type.

## Moral Qualities

*Amiability* is best expressed by the slope and softly rounded curves of the handwriting, though it is often found in the more energetic types. Here the turns of the letters will be

The capitals and the rounded curves are clear indications of kindness of heart and tenderness.

found rounded, while the hand maintains its general angularity. Tenderness, amiability in excess, is shown by the flowing curves and slope of the whole hand and capitals that conform to this general indication.

*Candour* is indicated by an open, rounded hand, of even quality, and generally straight lines across the page. There is a plainness and a frankness in the form of the letter which expresses this quality very obviously.

*Conscientiousness* follows much the same lines as candour. Punctuation is well-marked, and there is an evidence of attention to detail throughout. Frequently, the more brilliant intellectual qualities are missing from this type of hand, but in some cases other fine qualities of the head as well as of the heart will be readily determined.

*Economy*, which passes by almost insensible gradations into miserliness and avarice, is distinguished by the shortened finals of the letters and a general sense of carefulness in the formation of the letters themselves. The handwriting is usually of the angular type. There is no spreading out of this hand, broadcast over the paper, or large flowing initials. The whole handwriting indicates forethought and care. An exaggeration of these indications of carefulness show the

gradation to avarice. Even the ascenders and descenders, in letters like *l* and *t* and *g* and *y*, are shortened as though to avoid waste of ink and paper.

*Generosity*, as might be expected, reverses the indications above. Particularly is this seen in the case of the finals. These turn well up and round. The *y* final is allowed a broad spreading curve, and the capitals are of like proportions. Generosity is usually allied with tenderness, though not always so. When it is coupled with affection the hand is well sloped and curved.

*Humility* is betrayed by a small writing, free from ostentation and flourish.

*Melancholy* shows the exact reversal of ambition, and usually of energy also, in the descending character of the line of writing. There is generally an absence of the typically selfish characteristics. The writing is more rounded, is inclined to the indolent and apathetic, though sometimes it may exhibit vitality and power.

*Pride.*—The usual signs in the handwriting are that of a large-sized letter with capitals that emphasize it. There

Mark Twain's Signature, shown above, is a splendid example of self-assertiveness.

will generally be a good form to these and probably a flourish beneath the signature.

*Sensuousness.*—A typical adjunct to many painters and some writers. It is generally marked by the heaviness of the line of the signature. As was explained in the delineations of some of the great painters and writers, sensuousness, the love of beauty, must not be confused with its antithesis in excess, sensuality. In the latter the heaviness is unrelieved. In the former there is always some gradation in line strength.

*Selfishness* is indicated by angularity and compression of the handwriting. A rounded style of letter, although it may be compressed, is not an indication of selfishness. When the letter is very pronounced there is a tendency apparent in the

initials to reverse the ordinary curve. Selfishness may also be indicated in a writing that is otherwise capable of showing affection by the inversion of curve of capitals.

*Tact* is usually associated with a fine-lined handwriting, tending to the upright, but small and with spear-shaped loops to the *l* and *h*, a straightness of line and a final that extends without much rise to it.

*Vanity* is a quality that is easily identified in the ornate, and frequently otherwise unmeaning, flourish beneath the signature. The capitals, too, tend to exaggeration in form and over-elaboration.

---

# FORTUNES IN FACES

We are all attracted to some faces and repelled by others. Leaving out mere prettiness and good looks from the question, we instinctively find that this person's face inspires confidence, whilst someone else's makes no impression on us at all. Thus, we read faces hardly without knowing it.

But, however well we are able to sum up an individual, intuitively, by his face and features, it is highly important that we should know why we applaud one and feel aversion for another. Therefore, let us study the subject of faces, and deal with them analytically.

Generally speaking, a face should be mapped out in three portions about equal. The brow should form the uppermost third part ; the entire length of the nose, the second portion, and the distance from the bottom of the nose to the chin the remaining space. As a matter of fact, the middle or nose portion is often the least of these three divisions.

Now, when a face conforms to these dimensions, you have an individual who belongs to the rank and file of England. He is ordinary in, of course, a satisfactory sense ; he will work well, he will play well, he is patriotic, he will settle down and marry when the time comes, and he will do all the things which an ordinary citizen will do by nature. He is not meant to be a leader of men ; he will not be a Selfridge nor a Winston Churchill. He will just get on with his job and life, his and make an ordinary success of them. them.

Suppose now that we are confronted with an individual whose brow is very much shorter than, say, his nose or his chin. Very likely the tip of his nose comes about half way down his entire face. It is an absolute certainty that this individual cannot be intellectual nor would he be of any use where deep thinking was required. He might be a good and willing worker, but it would be useless to set him a problem or to put him in charge of others.

On the other hand, suppose the individual has a deep brow, taking up more than a third of his facial length. This is a good sign. Your man will be an alert and quick thinker, one who sees things before they happen ; he will be a captain over others, and the extent of his abilities will be governed by the extent of his brow, leaving out, of course, cases which are beyond normality.

Turning to the area occupied by the nose, it is a good sign when this is long rather than short. A small nose belongs to a person with a narrow outlook on life, and some people even go so far as to say they would never trust a person with such a nose. Large noses are an indication of large-hearted natures ; but if coming to a point, a business brain is indicated. A thin bridge suggests a refined nature, but it may be cold and calculating as well. The *retroussé* nose, tilted up at the tip, usually belongs to someone who is a shade conceited, who, probably knows a good deal of other people's business, but who is bright and excellent company. A rounded, fleshy tip, though by no means beautiful, is a sure sign of a kindly nature.

The third portion of the face, that devoted to the mouth and chin, is best when given neither more or less than its due proportion. A small chin, for instance, generally betokens a person of little character and, if receding, it shows a nature that is easily swayed by the wills of others. A prominent chin, when viewed sideways, is a clear indication of strong character and a forceful nature ; but this must not be confused

with the deep, flat chin which indicates a vain and shallow person, one who will waver when faced with difficulties.

Much may, of course, be learnt from the mouth. When large it suggests kindness, but if the lips are thick there is a lack of refinement as well. Small mouths go with an uncharitable nature, and there is a form of " pursed-up " small mouth which belongs to people who will pick you to pieces, without any doubt. The mouth that turns down at the ends may show a cold, calculating nature, but it will be eminently just, whatever else happens. If the lips end with a short vertical line or crease, the possessor has a contented nature and a strong character.

Of eyes, the colour means very little and it would be unsafe to draw any conclusions from it. However, a good deal may be learnt from the shape, position and habits of the eyes. Small, beady eyes are those of a heartless, unfeeling person ; when set too close together, they are likely to suggest dishonesty, but let them be large and wide open and you have, for sure, a kindly nature, one that will go out of its way to do somebody a good turn. Long narrow eyes are found with natures which see much, but say little. You never know how they will sum you up. As is well known, the eyes that seldom look directly at you are those of a " shifty " individual and, should the eyes waver and blink, it is a sign that determination is lacking. For preference select the steady eye that looks without piercing, that is large and not too wide open, that has a few kindly creases below it, close to the nose. Here you have a man or woman who will stand by you till the last day.

Turning to the ears, it may be affirmed that slightly small ears show culture and a refined nature : very small ones are indicative of a person lacking in character. On the other hand, large ears are a sign of a good nature, but it may be of the rough and ready type. Long but narrow ears plainly show the artistic temperament which cannot tolerate anything that is ordinary and commonplace. It has been said that a fleshy lobe is a sign that the possessor has an unusual amount of love and admiration for small children.

Now as to hair. Dark brown hair is the best where energy and force are concerned. If it is straight, the possessor is likely to be of even temper and reliable ; if curly, the man is chivalrous, and the woman needs a partner to escort her through life.

Light brown hair is a sign of a nice, kind nature, perhaps a little " easy-going." Light brown haired people, however, are not usually among the world's thinkers.

Very light brown hair, almost cream coloured, is a sign in women of fickleness.

Red hair is, usually, associated with vigour and, sometimes, conceit. Possessors of such hair are a little fiery in love matters, and their tempers are not equable. This is especially the case when the red is not a pure red, but is streaked with brown, or when the pure red is combined with brown eyebrows.

Straight black hair betokens a character that is more ambitious than charitable, while curly black hair shows the man or woman who has a love for amusements.

Coarse hair on an unruly head that persists in being untidy shows a person who is born to do great things. He or she is not going to take a back seat.

Fine, silky hair, on the other hand, suggests that the individual will do just what he is told and has little desire to be a leader.

Finally, the long-haired man is a man of moods. He has ideas that are seldom practicable and he will not make his way in the world in any of the ordinary channels.

# HOW TO READ HEADS

It is very interesting to make a study of heads, just as it is of faces. Both give very accurate readings of the characters, the qualities and the failings of the possessors. Some of the qualities of a head, you may read at a glance, but others are only revealed by actually touching the parts and assessing their proportions. The former can be applied by you without the knowledge of the individual concerned, but the latter requires his or her co-operation.

Phrenology, the name given to the science of reading character as revealed by the shape of the head, can be made a life-study. There is much to learn and the various applications are numerous; but a great deal may be grasped in a few minutes and, for the average person, all that need be known is set down here.

The science is based on the fact that the brain rules our actions, our character and all that makes us individuals. Moreover, each part of the brain has its special work and duties. Thus, if any part is highly developed, the qualities attributed to that part will be highly developed. Similarly, if any portion is hardly apparent, those qualities will be, practically, non-existent. And, of course, a medium development will suggest a moderate possession of the qualities.

From this, it will be seen that all that is now necessary is for you to be able to recognise the various areas of the head, and to know for what they stand. The diagram will help as far as the first is concerned, and the descriptions, which follow, will make the second quite clear.

1. The Amative Centre.—Indicates amativeness, instinct of sexual love, affection.

2. The Parental Centre.—Indicates a desire for and love of offspring and all young.

3. The Gregarious Centre.—Indicates a desire for friendships, sociability, and a love of other people's company.

4. The Inhabitive Centre.—Love of home and country.

5. The Concentrative Centre.—Indicates a methodical character, not appreciative of changes.

6. The Combative Centre.—Indicates courage and resistance.

7. The Executive Centre.—Indicates energy and the power to command others.

8. The Alimentive Centre.—Indicates an appreciation of good foods ; one who eats for the pleasure of eating.

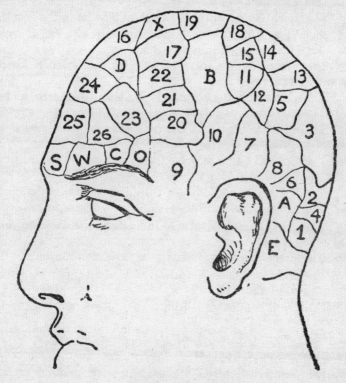

**A Map of the Head.**

9. The Acquisitive Centre.—A desire to collect things.

10. The Secretive Centre.—Indicates the power of self-restraint ; one who never speaks his mind openly.

11. The Watchful Centre.—Indicates cautiousness, guardedness, apprehensiveness of consequences.

12. The Approbative Centre.—Indicates a high regard for the opinions of others, and a love of praise.

13. The Self-Respective Centre.—Self-esteem, dignity, pride.

14. The Self-Assertive Centre.—Indicates perseverance, firmness and quick to make a decision.

15. The Justice Centre.—Indicates respect for the rights of others and a high regard for justice.

16. The Hope Centre.—Indicates a cheerful outlook on life, and one who hopes for the best.

17. The Spirituality Centre.—Indicates a belief in the occult.

18. The Veneration Centre.—Indicates one who has a high regard for the good qualities of others.

19. The Sympathetic Centre.—Indicates benevolence, kindness and sympathy.

20. The Constructive Centre.—Indicates a desire to make things, to put things together.

21. The Ideal Centre.—Indicates a love of the beautiful, a poetic nature.

22. The Imitative Centre.—Indicates a faculty for imitating others, mimicry, alertness to copy.

23. The Mirth-Loving Centre.—Indicates a sense of humour.

24. The Comparison Centre.—Faculty for discernment.

25. The Eventuality Centre.—Indicates a veneration for all that is old.

26. The Tune Centre.—Indicates a love for music.

A. The Pairing Centre.—Indicates a desire for conjugal love, oneness of affection.

B. The Sublime Centre.—Indicates a love of all that is majestic and grand.

C. The Colour Centre.—Indicates a sense for colour.

D. The Suavity Centre.—Indicates geniality, blandness.

E. The Vitative Centre.—Indicates a love to hold on to life ; death and disease-resisting instincts.

O. The Order Centre.—Indicates a perception of method.

S. The Size Centre.—Well-balanced sense of proportion.

W. The Weight Centre.—Indicates a perception of distances, of weights and a skill, in reckoning up sizes and values.

X. The Charitable Centre.—Indicates a charitable nature ; often merged with No. 19.

# FORTUNE TELLING BY CARDS

Almost as soon as civilisation began, people used playing-cards to tell fortunes. Naturally, there are many methods which can be employed for the purpose : some are wonderfully clever and others are less so. We have made a study of countless old documents and have consulted a number of people who have made a life study of card-lore, and the methods which follow are the result of this research.

## The Pack and Its Significance

Before describing any of the accepted methods, it is advisable to say a few words about the pack and its significance.

The normal pack consists of fifty-two cards—four suits of thirteen each. But, in fortune-telling, it is only occasionally that more than thirty-two cards are used. The pack then consists of the cards ranging from the ace to the seven. In other words, the sixes, fives, fours, threes and twos of all the four suits are set aside.

Each card has a generally accepted meaning, and every one of these meanings is set out below. It will be noted that, not only is a regular reading given for each card, but a reversed reading is furnished as well. Exactly what a reversed card is, puzzles many people, so let us explain. Suppose that the pack is shuffled and a number of cards are dealt out, face upwards, or perhaps some cards are laid out in formation on the table. It will be seen that certain of them are turned upside down. This will be very noticeable in the case of the Ace of Spades, and less apparent in many other instances. But, before the pack took on its present design, all court cards and most of the others had a proper and a reversed appearance, according to which way they were set down. As many cards are now designed to be viewed both ways, it is impossible to set them down in a reversed sense. So as not to lose the reversed property, the usual plan is to mark the top left-hand corner of every card, and to reckon the setting as reversed

when the dot comes at the bottom right-hand corner. Of course, the dot must be placed on such cards as can still be reversed to agree with the proper way-up of the design.

Here are the meanings of the various cards:

## HEART VALUES.

ACE.—Good news, a house, a love letter; *reversed*, disappointment, removal, or a friendly visit.

KING.—Kind-hearted, loving man of fair complexion; *reversed*, an uncertain, inconstant lover.

QUEEN.—A generous, loving woman, fair; *reversed*, crossed in love and capricious.

JACK.—A pleasure-loving bachelor, a friend or lover; *reversed*, a lover with a grievance.

TEN.—Good fortune and happiness; *reversed*, changes, a birth.

NINE.—Success, the wish card; *reversed*, passing troubles.

EIGHT.—Love, invitations, thoughts of marriage; *reversed*, unreciprocated affection, jealousy.

SEVEN.—Contentment and favours; *reversed*, boredom and jealousy.

## DIAMOND VALUES.

ACE.—Marriage offer, ring, bank notes; *reversed*, demand for debt, bad news.

KING.—Fair or grey-haired man, widower; *reversed*, treachery and deceit.

QUEEN.—Fair woman, widow, a gossip; *reversed*, untrustworthy, a flirt.

JACK.—An official, a messenger; *reversed*, mischief-maker.

TEN.—Journey or removal, finance; *reversed*, misfortune.

NINE.—Anxiety, news; *reversed*, danger, family quarrels.

EIGHT.—Amorous, short journey; *reversed*, affections ignored.

SEVEN.—Child, unfriendly criticism; *reversed*, scandal, minor successes.

## CLUB VALUES.

ACE.—Good luck, papers or letters bringing in money, or good news; *reversed*, ill news, delayed letter.

KING.—A dark man, friendly and straight; *reversed*, worries and slight troubles.

QUEEN.—Dark woman, affectionate ; *reversed*, undependable, perplexities.

JACK.—Athlete, clever, good lover ; *reversed*, luck may change.

TEN.—Ease and prosperity, journey, luck ; *reversed*, sea voyage, estrangement.

NINE.—Legacy ; *reversed*, obstacles.

EIGHT.—The love of a dark man or woman, joy and good luck in consequence ; *reversed*, documents causing trouble, litigation.

SEVEN.—Success with money ; *reversed*, financial worries and losses.

### SPADE VALUES.

ACE.—Satisfaction in love, high building ; *reversed*, sorrow, death, disappointments.

KING.—Widower, untrustworthy lawyer ; *reversed*, a very dangerous enemy, impending evil.

QUEEN.—Widow, faithful friend ; *reversed*, intrigue, treacherous woman.

JACK.—Doctor or barrister, bad mannered ; *reversed*, deceitful, traitor.

TEN.—Long journey, grief ; *reversed*, slight sickness.

NINE.—Failure, financial or domestic ; *reversed*, death of dear friend.

EIGHT.—Impending illness, sorrow ; *reversed*, rejected affection, evil living, quarrels.

SEVEN.—A change for the worse, a resolution ; *reversed*, accidents or losses.

Having noted the meaning of each card, we will now see how to invoke the aid of the pack.

# The Past, Present and Future

The pack of thirty-two cards must be well shuffled by the enquirer and cut with the left hand into two heaps, which can be as equal or unequal in size as the enquirer fancies.

After the cut, the two heaps must not be placed together again until the top card of each has been laid aside, face downwards to form the usual Surprise. The remaining cards are then squared up and dealt into three heaps of ten cards, which represent respectively the Past (left-hand heap), the Present (centre), and the Future (right-hand heap).

The ten cards of the first heap—the Past—should be spread

in a row from left to right and then examined for pairs, triplets, and quadruplets, according to our Table of Meanings. You should carefully note all reversed cards as they tend to lessen the good predicted, or increase the evil, as the case may be. Such cards usually refer to opportunities lost. It is also very helpful to notice which suit predominates in each heap, Clubs being the most fortunate and Spades the most evil. This predominance of colour shows whether the greater amount of success has been reached by the enquirer or is still to come.

After this the cards should be read singly, by their several meanings, from right to left of the row.

When all these have been thrown aside, the centre heap, representing the Present, is similarly examined and then the Future.

Finally, the Surprise is consulted to see what unexpected event is going to influence the life and fortunes of the enquirer.

# The Four Aces

This is a very simple method for determining a single question or wish. The thirty-two cards are well shuffled by the enquirer—the diviner then deals off thirteen cards, face upwards, on to the table, and makes a careful search for the four Aces. If any are found, place them, face up, by themselves. The remainder of the pack, including what are left of the thirteen, are then re-shuffled as before, and the diviner again deals out thirteen cards and searches for further Aces.

This can be done for a third time, but that is all. The earlier the four Aces appear, the better it will be for the enquirer—if in the first deal, it is exceptionally fortunate ; if in the second, it is certainly very good luck—as a rule, they are not completed till the third attempt has been made.

Those that appear in each deal should be kept separate, as it is very important to notice the order in which the suits appear. This will clearly show the amount of effort needed before the wish or question is satisfactorily answered—for instance, if the Spade Ace appears first of all, the enquirer must be prepared to face trouble and difficulty, even should all four Aces appear in the course of the first deal.

This is a very useful method to know, as several questions can be dealt with in a very short time. It is as well to limit the questions to three, however, as the cards are never so reliable when overworked, or tired.

Another simple method for answering a single question is worked with the full pack of fifty-two cards. First remove the type card representing the enquirer, King or Queen as it happens to be (*see* below). Then have the fifty-one cards well shuffled and cut into three heaps of any size. They should be cut towards the right by the left hand—the enquirer makes the first cut, placing the upper portion of the pack on the right and then cuts this latter heap into two.

The diviner takes the centre heap (originally the middle of the pack) face down in his hand, adds to it the right-hand heap (originally the top of the pack), and finally the left-hand heap goes on top of all. Now make a circle of forty-two cards, face down, on the table—inside this make a triangle of the remaining nine cards.

The enquirer must now turn over any fifteen cards, replacing them, face upwards, in the original positions. When this is done, read them according to the number of each suit exposed.

The Type Card is as follows :

The King or Queen of Diamonds is the type card for men or women with light colouring, blue or grey eyes, flaxen or red hair, also grey and white hair.

The King or Queen of Hearts is the type card for men or women who are fair, though not so light as for Diamonds. Blue or grey eyes and brown hair.

The King or Queen of Clubs is the type card for men or women who have brown eyes and darkish brown hair.

The King or Queen of Spades is the type for men or women who are dark complexioned, with dark eyes and hair.

## The Seven Answers

The thirty-two cards are shuffled and cut once, as usual with the left hand, and the enquirer should wish once during this process.

Then the cards are dealt out, one by one, so as to form seven heaps—six of these to form a semi-circle—the cards for these being placed face downwards while the seventh heap is built in the centre and the cards are dealt face upwards.

The seven packs represent " yourself " (i.e., the enquirer) ; " your home " ; " what you expect " ; " what you don't expect " ; " the Surprise " ; " what is sure to come true " ; and " your wish."

It will be at once noticed that some heaps will contain five cards each, others only four each. The heaps should be arranged from left to right—the first card dealt starting the heap on the extreme left and the seventh card going, face upwards, in the centre.

Some diviners employ this method, but only use seventeen cards—the pack is shuffled and cut as before, but only the first seventeen cards are dealt. This method is certainly simpler, as the heaps only contain two or three cards each ; it is also thought to be a great advantage, as the exposed cards naturally vary greatly as regards the proportion from each suit. If you use the full pack, there must of necessity be eight of each suit ; whereas if only seventeen are dealt, six or seven or even eight of one suit might appear on the table, and it is obvious that the preponderance of any suit would greatly affect the reading.

Some diviners object to the seven packs, maintaining that it is false art to have one heap for " what you don't expect," and another for " the Surprise." The sixth heap is also rather feeble, and certainly looks as if it had originally been included to make the number uneven. This school of diviners therefore deal off thirteen cards only from the full pack of thirty-two, and build up only five heaps for " yourself " ; " your home " ; " what you expect " ; " the Surprise " ; and " your wish."

# Divination by Obstacles

Have the pack of thirty-two cards well shuffled and cut once only. Pick out the type card representing the enquirer and hold the rest of the pack face downwards in your hand. The type card is placed in the centre of the table, the top card from the pack is turned over and placed above the type card, the second card being similarly placed below. The third is now placed on the left and the fourth card on the right. The fifth card is placed upon the type card, covering it. The diviner now discards eight cards altogether, and, that being done, adds another card to each of the five in the same order as before—above, below, left, right, and upon the type card.

The lay-out being completed, take an ace, two, three, four and five of any suit from another pack and shuffle them. Then, the five cards are held, face down to the enquirer who selects any one he likes. Whichever card he takes indicates

by its number the pair of cards which provide his divination. Thus the ace indicates the centre pair, while the two, three, four and five indicate the pairs as numbered in the illustration. To read the meaning of the selected pair, the list at the commencement of this chapter is consulted.

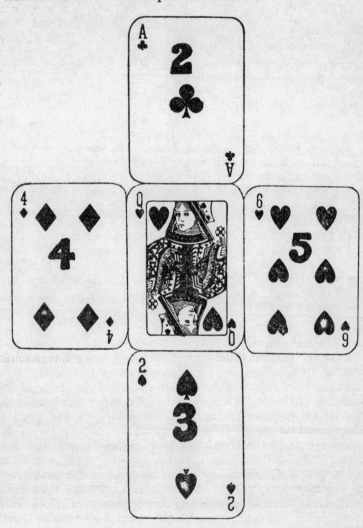

DIVINATION BY OBSTACLES
The Order for Laying the first five Cards

# Divination by Nines

The pack of thirty-two cards is thoroughly shuffled, and then the person whose fate is being determined draws a card from it, at random. After noting the suit, the card is replaced in the pack and a fresh shuffling is made.

That done, the pack is cut by the individual concerned, the left hand being used, and the next thing is for him to set out the cards in three horizontal rows of nine and a final row of five. Each now must be begun from the right and completed by the left-hand card.

Now that the thirty-two cards are set out, the card taken at random from the pack is recalled and the King or Queen of the same suit is found in the " lay-out "—the King, if a man is consulting his fortunes ; the Queen, if it is a lady.

Having found the King or Queen, as the case requires, count nine, eighteen and twenty-seven from it and pick out the three cards indicated. The counting follows the order in which the cards were laid ; it may be necessary to go beyond the thirty-second card and continue with the first.

The significance of the three cards is read in accordance with the meanings given earlier. It must be recognised that the second card is more powerful than the first, and the third more than the second. Thus, the third card may contradict the second or first, though these would necessarily rob the third of some of its force.

# The Star of Fifteen

Take the pack of thirty-two cards and select the type card, placing it face upwards in the centre of the table. The enquirer must now well shuffle the pack and cut it once only with the left hand. Take the pack and spread it out fan-wise and let the enquirer choose fifteen cards, one by one, placing them one by one, and face downwards, in a heap by themselves. Discard the remaining cards and pick up the chosen fifteen, holding them face upwards.

Place the first card to the left of the type card, representing the enquirer ; the second card to the right ; the third card goes above, and the fourth card below, thus forming a simple cross. The fifth card is now placed upon the type card itself.

Repeat this process with five more cards, thus increasing the size of your cross—and again with the final five cards.

The type card will now have three cards on each of the four sides ; while the fifth, tenth, and fifteenth cards will have been placed upon the type card itself, covering it.

Now take each set of three cards by itself and read their meaning according to the table, being specially careful to watch for reversed cards as well as for pairs and triplets. Also carefully note if two or more of the three cards are of any one suit, as that greatly affects the result.

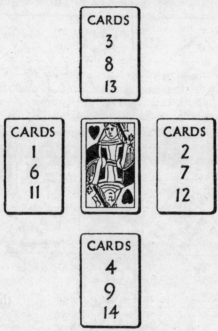

THE STAR OF FIFTEEN
Cards 5, 10 and 15 are placed upon the centre of the Star

The set of three cards on the left should be read first of all, as they represent the immediate past of the enquirer ; then the set of three on the right which govern the immediate future.

After these, if it is wished, you can read the three cards of the upper set, which show the more remote past and which, consequently, are somewhat affected by your reading of the left-hand set. Balancing one set carefully against the other

you should be easily able to decide if things are improving for your enquirer—or if they are drifting for the reverse.

Now consider the bottom set of three cards, which refer to the more remote future, and, after reading their meaning, noting reverses, pairs, triplets, and suits as before, you must balance these against the right-hand set and thus determine which way the future will tend. Suppose, for instance, that apart from their individual meanings, there are two Spades

THE SIMPLE STAR

in the right-hand set and either one or no Spade in the bottom set, then the enquirer may certainly look forward cheerfully to a lessening of any difficulties that may be facing him at the moment.

The central set of three, covering the type card, gives your answer to any special wish or question of the enquirer's— they do not apply to the past or future and therefore need not be read as regards their individual meanings. Go by the suit colours, making any necessary allowance for the presence of two or three cards of the same value.

# The Simple Star

Another star formation makes use of fifteen cards. To tell the fortune in this method, place the significator first of all on the centre position marked C (consultant).

Shuffle the cards as previously directed, and let the consultant cut the pack into three. The cards thus cut are to be turned up and used as the basis for the drawing for the star. From the centre portion of the pack take the first card thus exposed and place it upon 1. From the left-hand portion of the pack take the top card for 2. From the right-hand portion of the pack the card for 3. The fourth card is taken from the centre portion, and so on until twelve have been drawn.

To determine the thirteenth and fourteenth cards, re-make the pack, and let the consultant shuffle and cut. Then take the top card of the bottom half for the thirteenth, and the bottom card of the top half for the fourteenth. These should be placed directly above the significator, as shown in the diagram.

These two cards are very important indications, and must be read finally as denoting what is likely very soon to come to pass. The general meanings of the cards may be used for the reading, with the modifications resulting from the positions as they come out.

# A Week's Happenings

The enquirer takes a pack and cuts it with the left hand, forming three heaps. The diviner now takes the top card of each heap, face downwards, and places them so as to start a row of fifteen cards, the top card of the left-hand heap being first removed. The cards are then re-shuffled and cut as before, the diviner again removing the top card from each heap and adding them to the row. This is repeated five times, so that fifteen cards, face downwards, are ranged on the table from left to right.

The diviner now turns over, face upwards, the extreme card at either end and reads the meaning which applies to the following day. Clubs are very fortunate ; Hearts are quite good ; Diamonds are of fair portent ; but Spades are unlucky.

In many cases the inner meaning of the cards is never

considered at all, this method being used on the Continent to determine, simply and solely, which will be the fortunate and unfortunate days in the week—Sunday counting as the first day, of course. Remember that a Spade on the right and a Club on the left would indicate that things would certainly go wrong in the early part of the day, but would rapidly improve after noon. Whereas a Club on the right and a Spade on the left would indicate a prosperous morning, followed by a calamitous afternoon and evening.

A WEEK'S HAPPENINGS
A Club on the right and a Spade on the left indicates a prosperous morning, followed by a calamitous afternoon and evening

Fourteen cards are turned up in this way, two and two, leaving the centre card face downwards on the table. The diviner should now note, on a slip of paper, the point values of each pair of cards, in case the enquirer should be confronted on that day by any business or other matter in which figures are concerned. For instance, if a Nine of Spades and a Seven of Hearts are the cards for the following Tuesday (the third day), then anything involving nine or any multiple of nine should be avoided, and those things involving seven should be followed up. Suppose anyone calls and wishes to make an appointment, fix the seventh, fourteenth, twenty-first, or twenty-eighth day of the month. Should the *seventh day* (*i.e.*, the next Tuesday) fall on the ninth, eighteenth, or twenty-seventh of the month, it would obviously be a bad day to select. In the same way, if the fourteenth, twenty-first, or twenty-eighth of the month were the ninth day following, that also would prove a bad day.

With all these particulars to help him, or her, along, your client should be able to avoid all mishaps and make the best use of the opportunities for good fortune that might come his, or her, way.

The fifteenth card is used to answer one question, which, in this case, must be a spoken one. The suit of the card determines whether the answer is to be " yes " ; " probably " ; " doubtful " ; or " no "—and the pip value should be noted if it can be made to fit in any way, as that particular number will have a fateful influence, one way or another, over the matter in question. Its influence, however, only lasts for the week in question, so if it is a Spade, it is wise to warn your client to delay and wait for a more propitious time before proceeding with the matter in hand.

# Wishes

Invite your friends to sit around the table, get out a pack of fifty-two playing cards, shuffle them thoroughly and deal them out, giving each person five cards. Place the remainder of the pack, if any, in the centre of the table. All cards must be kept face down until it is the turn of a player to turn one over.

The next thing is for each player to write a wish on a small piece of paper, to fold it into four, and to initial it on the outside. All the papers are collected by the dealer and placed in a box or other convenient receptacle.

Play commences with the individual on the dealer's left : he or she turns over the top card on his pack and, when it has been scrutinized, the person on his left turns over his top card. Subsequent players on the left of those who have already turned a card follow in their order, round and round the table.

Each card is scrutinized, as it appears, to see if the player's wish will be granted. It will be fulfilled if

(a) It is the nine of Hearts that is turned.

(b) The turned card is the next highest to the card turned by the previous player. Here it should be noted that twos are lowest and they follow in numerical order up to tens, followed by Jacks, Queens, Kings and Aces. It is not necessary for the higher card to belong to the same suit as the lower one.

(c) The exposed card and the card exposed immediately before, by the previous player, add up to seven.

As soon as a player turns a card that grants his or her wish, the dealer hands back the player's folded paper.

A successful player drops out of the game until the cards are shuffled and dealt again. For this, a fresh set of papers and wishes must be drawn up.

WISHES

Three sets of cards which signify that the wish will be granted.
(a) The nine of Hearts : (b) An Ace following a King and (c)
Two cards that add up to seven

# HOW THE MOON INFLUENCES YOU

The following information has been derived from a document some hundreds of years old :

The Moon exercises an influence over the children of men which varies with her monthly age, in the same way as the Sun affects people differently as it progresses through the Signs of the Zodiac. The fate of all children may be, thus, determined by noting in an almanack whether they are born during the first, second, third or fourth quarter of the Moon.

*Children born between the New Moon and the First Quarter* are likely to thrive and live to a good age. If born within the first twenty-four hours, they will be exceptionally fortunate : if on the second day, they will have luck, sometimes of a remarkable character : if on the third day, they will make friends with people in high places and gain by such friendships : if on the fourth day, they will certainly be lucky, but will also suffer reverses : if on the fifth or sixth day, they will lose opportunities through pride : if on the seventh day, they must conceal their wishes, should they hope for them to come true.

*Children born between the First Quarter and the Full Moon* are likely to rise above the station of their parents and have a happy life. If born on the first day, they will be able to prosper in business : if on the second day, theirs ought to be a life devoid of difficulties : if on the third day, they should gain wealth, but they may have to go far afield to find it : if on the fourth or fifth day, they will have an engaging manner and make many friends : if on the sixth day, their lot will lie in easy places : if on the seventh day, people will look up to them and welcome their advice.

*Children born between the Full Moon and the Last Quarter* will have many difficulties with which to contend, but the possession of considerable doggedness will generally help them to win through. If born on the first day, they will be more successful in other continents than their own : if on the second day, there is prosperity for them in the business world :

if on the third day, their successes will be heralded by very clear dreams : if on the fourth day, they will not know what dangers are : if on the fifth day, they should avoid taking unnecessary risks in money matters : if during the remainder of the quarter, they will be endowed with a strong constitution.

*Children born between the Last Quarter and the New Moon* will be affectionate and upright. If born on the first or second day, they will prefer the home to the outside world : if on the third day, they will be dependable in every way : if on the fourth day, they will be very sensitive to the troubles of others : if on the fifth day, they will be fortunate in matrimonial matters : if on the sixth day, they will be comforting children and ideal parents : if during the remainder of the quarter, they will acquire wealth more through being trustworthy than through skill.

# CRYSTAL-GAZING

There is no doubt that Crystal-gazing has produced some very remarkable results. In at least one instance, a baffling crime was solved by a seer looking into the Crystal and reconstructing the whole of the incidents. But, as far as we are concerned, Crystal-gazing is helpful, most, in depicting the future.

It must not be supposed that anyone can sit down, in any frame of mind, and, by gazing into a Crystal, obtain an answer or solution to some particular question. The Crystal is not so amenable as all that. What it will do is to reveal to a suitable seer facts on which his or her mind is intently set and about which he or she is puzzled.

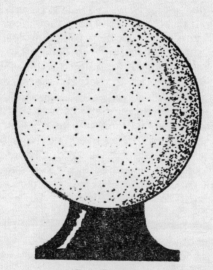

THE CRYSTAL

Should you be desirous of studying the art of Crystal-reading, your first step is to obtain a suitable Crystal. The publishers of this book can supply a very sensitive Crystal.

Regarding its use, daylight and artificial light are both

111

equally suitable, but if the former is used, a north light is best.

The observer should sit with his back to the light, holding the sphere in the palm of his hand, which may rest comfortably on the lap, or it can be placed on a table, with a stand under it, and a back screen of black velvet or dark material. The latter materially assists by cutting off side lights and reflections.

Steady gazing in complete silence is absolutely necessary, since the distraction of the ordinary attentions is a great hindrance. You must allow your mind to wander and become a blank. The crackling of a fire, for instance, will centre your mind on the burning coals and prevent its preparation for the occult phenomena.

We know that certain people are much more receptive than others : in fact, some are totally unreceptive. The chief difference between those who can and those who cannot delve into the Crystal's secrets is that the former can banish all extraneous thoughts from the mind, whilst the latter find this impossible.

Success is indicated when the sphere, ceasing to reflect, becomes milky, a clouded colour following (generally red, and its complement green), turning to blackness, which seems to roll away like a curtain, disclosing to the view of the gazer, pictures, scenes, figures in action, sentences of warnings, advice, etc.

The danger at this supreme moment is that the seer will be surprised into full waking consciousness. During the process of abstraction, which precedes every vision or series of visions, the consciousness of the seer is gradually and imperceptibly withdrawn from his surroundings. He forgets that he is seated in this or that room, that such a person may be at his right hand, such another at his left. He even forgets he is gazing into a Crystal. He hears nothing, sees nothing, save what is passing before the eyes of his soul. He loses sight, for the time, even of his own identity.

Therefore, when your vision is suddenly arrested by an apparition, startling in its reality and instantaneous production, even though hoped for and expected, the reaction is so violent and rapid that you may be carried back into full consciousness of your physical condition. Therefore, the qualifications of self-possession and confidence in your own soul-faculties are of primary importance.

# PALMISTRY

## What the Lines in Your Hands Denote

Would you know your real character, your capabilities, your faults and failings, and, most important of all, the probable outcome of your life ? If you desire to know all these things as certainly as day follows night, then study your hands. They are wonderful indications of your inner-self : they show by their texture, shape and markings every detail of your make-up ; and, just as two people are not exactly alike, so no two hands are exactly similar.

We will now deal with the various features of the hands.

## The Palms

If the palm is thin, skinny and narrow, it tells of one timid, weak-minded, with narrowness of views and paucity of intellect, as well as a want of depth of character, energy, mental and moral force. If accompanied with long thin fingers, it will indicate a tyrannical disposition.

If the palm is in proportion with the fingers and thumb and the general physique, firm without hardness, of elastic consistency* without flabbiness, it will indicate an evenly-balanced mind, ready to receive impressions, appreciative, intelligent and able to sustain and carry out the promptings of instinct. But if over-developed in its proportions, it will tend to produce over-confidence, selfishness and sensuality, especially if the development is towards the base of the hand.

If this hand is hard, with the palm longer than the fingers, the character will have a trend towards brutality and animal propensities, unless restrained by other indications, such as a strong thumb and a good head line.

The palm should be normal and in proportion to the thumb and fingers and the general physique, otherwise it indicates a modification of the signs on the rest of the hand.

If the palm is flabby and soft, it will indicate indolence, mental or physical, and a love of ease, luxury and pleasure ; opportunities will be missed from sheer laziness.

If thick and firm, while the colour is approaching white, there will be selfishness and coldness of disposition.

A hollow palm denotes misfortune, losses, unhappiness, and a prospect of failure in enterprises and undertakings.

# The Fingers and Finger Tips

Each finger is named from, and takes the quality of, the Mount under it. Thus the first, or index finger, is named Jupiter, the second finger is Saturn, the third is named Apollo, while the fourth, or little finger, is named Mercury. The thumb is not considered as a finger ; it is so important that it stands in a class by itself.

In examining the fingers, the first point to notice is their length. If any doubt is felt as to their length, let the subject close the fingers over the palm so as to ascertain how far towards the wrist they reach.

In practice, whenever the fingers extend anywhere below the centre of the Mount of Venus towards the wrist, they are classed as long, and long-fingered qualities are applied to them.

The tips of the fingers must, individually, be noted, and spatulate, square, conic or pointed qualities applied to the finger and its Mount. Fingers, to be well-balanced, should be set evenly on the palm, as, if low set, the strength of the Mount is reduced, while a high-set finger increases the strength of its Mount.

You must also note whether the fingers are close together at their base, or if there is a space between them. If the space between the thumb and the side of the hand is very wide, it will indicate one who is generous, a lover of freedom and independence, and who chafes under restraint. The fingers of Jupiter and Saturn separating widely show a carelessness of conventionalism. The fingers of Saturn and Apollo being widely separated show one careless as to the future, and with a trend to extravagance. The fingers of Apollo and Mercury widely separated indicate independence in action, one who will do as he or she wishes, regardless of what others may think.

When you find all the fingers widely separated, you may expect free thought, Bohemianism, and freedom of action. If all the fingers lie bunched together, you will have an individual difficult to get acquainted with, very stiff, stingy and self-centred.

Finger tips are classed as spatulate, i.e. broad and flat-

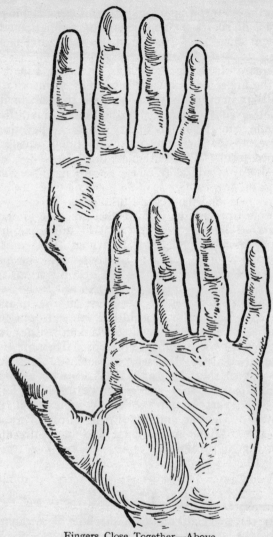

Fingers Close Together—Above
Fingers Separated—-Below

looking, square, conic or rounded, or pointed, according as they appear to the eye.

The Spatulate tip is the broadest ; its possessor always seeks the practical and commonsense side of things, and

is ever on the go, inspiring others with enthusiasm and activity. He is fond of sports, manual exercises, animals, and makes an excellent emigrant. He is a strong lover and is constant and true.

The Square tip is one which is distinctly square at the ends of the fingers, and indicates order, system, arrangement and regularity in everything. Disorder is to them an abomination, whether in the home, shop or office. They think and act by rule, and love punctuality in all. They are polite, strict observers of social customs, and resent any breach of accustomed forms. In addition to the foregoing, the Square tips are skilful in all games where precision and accuracy are an essential ; hence they are often good shots, as well as being careful in dress, and methodical in habits.

The Conic tip in shape forms a distinct cone at the end of the fingers. It reveals a nature artistic, impulsive, intuitive, quick and impressionable, one to whom the beautiful and harmonious strongly appeal. To these tips the precision, regularity and punctuality of the Square tip is a nuisance and a restraint.

Conic tips possess talent, quickness of mind, and great intuitiveness—this natural intuition, though one of their greatest gifts, is also an element of danger, as they are often led by it against the dictates of reasons. They are emotional and sympathetic, easily influenced, and as a result, they are not constant in their love affairs.

Pointed tips once seen, can never be mistaken for others, as their long, narrow and excessively pointed build cannot be forgotten. There is nothing of a practical nature in these Pointed tips ; all is inspirational and idealistic, and their possessors live in dreamland.

# The Length of the Fingers

Fingers can be relatively long, short or of medium length. Naturally, the latter are met most frequently.

The Long-fingered person is one who goes closely into details, accepts nothing as a whole, is very careful in small things, but often allows large ones to pass unnoticed, and is always more or less suspicious and easily offended. He is careful in all things, very sensitive, and neat in appearance. As a rule he possesses a good memory and makes a good

book-keeper ; in fact in any office where accuracy and attention to detail is essential he is at home.

It is not surprising to find that a person with long fingers is unsympathetic, cold-blooded, and by no means anxious to grant favours, nor are they always true to the affections.

The next type to be considered will be the Short fingers. These are found among all classes and in both sexes. Short fingers will scarcely reach to the centre of the Mount of Venus, but they may vary in degree of shortness according to the length of the palm. The shorter they are the more pronounced are their qualities.

The qualities of Short fingers are the reverse of Long ones. They think quickly, and if very short, like a flash, and act accordingly. They are highly intuitive, and quickly judge whether you are telling the truth or not. No question of analysis or detail troubles them. Things as a whole are what they deal with. They are impulsive and act on the spur of the moment ; they run the risk of making mistakes through jumping to conclusions. Hot-headed, and once started, they push diligently their enterprises.

Short-fingered people are only satisfied when doing big things—they build huge buildings and bridges, plan gigantic enterprises, lead armies, control large concerns, but leave details to long-fingers. They are as a rule quick-witted and very concise in their expressions, and have the faculty of saying much in little.

Naturally, the medium-lengthed fingers betoken people who have the above characteristics in a much modified form.

# The Thumb

The thumb is divided into three phalanges, just as the fingers are, and each stands for definite characteristics.

The special attributes of the first is will-power, determination and ability to command others. The second stands for reason and logic, perception and judgment ; whilst the third reveals the extent of love, sympathy and passion.

In order to note the details of the thumb, have the hands held up with the palms towards you, so that you are able to see whether the thumb is set high on the side of the hand, whether low, or in a medium position—the higher the thumb is set in the hand, the lower the grade of intelligence and the less the adaptability possessed by the owner. If the thumb

is set low, the wider it will open from the side of the hand. This low-set thumb will indicate a nature full of the highest human qualities and shows generosity, a love of liberty, independence and a readiness to lend a helping hand to others.

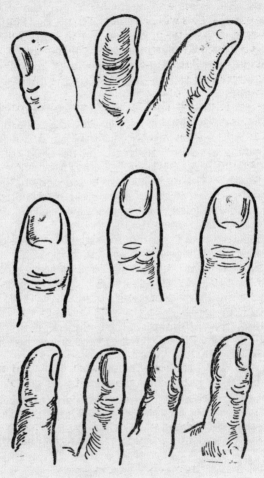

Various Types of Thumbs

If the thumb is short it will reduce the good qualities of its low setting considerably ; but this short low-set thumb is somewhat rare and will not be met with often.

Now, as to the shape :

THE ELEMENTARY.—This is an almost shapeless thumb, and has the appearance of a piece of flesh just stuck on the hand, without any regard to symmetry, and the two joints do not show where they separate. Its very appearance tells of heaviness, coarseness and animalism.

THE NERVOUS.—This will be recognised by its flat appearance —it looks as if it had been subject to heavy pressure ; such thumbs have all kinds of tips. As a rule they are soft and flabby, but it is the flat appearance which marks them. This thumb shows that the nervous force, and nervous energy, are too strong for its owner.

THE BROAD THUMB.—This thumb is not round or shapeless as the Elementary, nor has it the flat appearance of the Nervous thumb—on the contrary, if viewed from the back, or nailed side, it has a broad look in both phalanges and bears a strong and healthy appearance. It tells of strong determination, well supported by physical strength. It indicates the determination which succeeds, for it is pushing and aggressive.

THE STRONG THUMB.—This will appear to be of equal thickness throughout its whole length, yet delicate, shapely, with Conic or Square tip. The nail should be smooth and of good colour. It shows strength of will, the first phalanx being good, and with sound reasoning and logical qualities, the second phalanx being equally strong. It tells of a very diplomatic mind, firm determination, and a refined intelligent nature, yet with plenty of firmness of purpose, and gives refinement of will, intelligent reasoning, taste, tact, and perseverance.

THE PADDLE-SHAPED THUMB.—In this thumb, which is often seen, the Will phalanx is broad when looked at from the nail side, but it is not thick throughout. It is not thin or flat enough to be classed as a Nervous thumb. It shows strong determination, which, if the development is excessive, will tend to tyranny and obstinacy ; it is always a strong phalanx —even if it is deficient in length, the paddle shape gives it strength.

THE FLEXIBLE THUMB.—Bends back at the joint and marks one as extravagant, a spendthrift, brilliant, versatile, sentimental, generous and sympathetic, emotional and extremist. Square tips, a good Head line, and developed Mount of Saturn are needed to give the owner some necessary ballast.

THE STIFF THUMB.—This carries itself erect and close to the side of the hand, and indicates the possession of a practical

turn of mind, with commonsense ; economical and parsi-
monious. Quiet, cautious, plodding, reliable, but of a grasping
nature.

THE CLUBBED THUMB.—This is a thumb once seen never
forgotten. It has a Will phalanx, thick and round, or broad
with a short nail of coarse structure—in fact, the Will phalanx
has the appearance of a badly shaped ball. It shows terrific
obstinacy, and, in a bad hand, an ungovernable temper. It
is a warning of danger of bad temper underlying, and always
indicates intense obstinacy under opposition.

GENERALLY.—Large thumbs strengthen smooth fingers,
small thumbs increase the impulsiveness. Large thumbs
decrease the artistic qualities of Conic and Pointed tips by
making them more practical ; small thumbs make them
dreamy and listless. Large thumbs drive Square or Spatulate
tips to increased activity on practical lines ; small thumbs
make these tips mere talkers, not doers.

# The Finger Nails

Finger nails tell the palmist a great deal, since matters of
health and occupation are considerably bound up with the
condition and shape of the nails.

The nail should be smooth and pliable, but not brittle,
and should be pink as to its colour. The flutings or ridgings
of the nail, from the top to the base, indicate a nervous disorder ;
if serious, there will also be a brittle condition of the nail
and a marked tendency to grow away from the fingers.

The white flecks or spots often seen on the nails are the
first indication of approaching nerve trouble ; as the disorder
grows, the flecks enlarge, then coalesce, until the whole nail
is clouded with them—then fluting or ridging becomes more
pronounced, the nail grows brittle and begins to turn back
from the end and lose its shape. At this stage there is grave
danger ; the delicacy of the nerves becomes marked, and there
may even be danger of paralysis.

A NARROW NAIL shows one who does not possess robust
health but carries on by nervous energy. As a matter of fact,
it is the Psychic nail, and the delicacy of the psychic character
is present, rather than muscular health, such as is shown by
the broad nail. The narrow nail may be either white, yellow,
blue or pink, but never red—very often a blue colour will be
seen at its base, denoting poor circulation of the blood.

THE SHORT NAIL.—This tells of a critical turn of the mind, but if not very short, it will be more of the nature of investigation. The extremely short nail, flat, with the skin growing on it, shows pugnacity and an argumentative disposition. Add to this nail knotty fingers, a big thumb and hard hands, with the Mounts of Mars well developed, and a most pugnacious and disagreeable person will be the result.

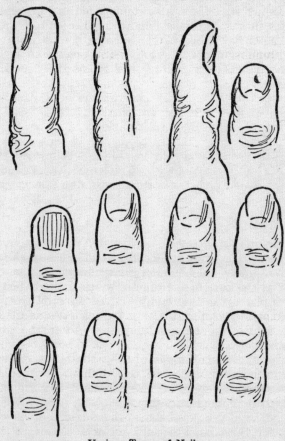

Various Types of Nails

OPEN AND FRANK NAILS.—These are broad at the tip, curve round the finger, broadening at the base and pink in colour. They reveal a nature open and frank, to whom

honesty of thought is natural. They are broad open-looking nails, and their breadth shows the broad views and ideas of their owners—this is especially so if they are pink in colour.

SQUARE-ENDED NAILS.—These taper towards the base, and are often seen on long fingers—this is an indication of heart trouble, and these nails are found on all shapes of fingers or hands ; the nail is small and often of a deep blue colour at the base, and shows structural weakness of the heart.

BULBOUS NAIL.—This is so pronounced in its shape, that, once seen, it can never be forgotten. The end of the finger as well as the nail has to be taken in conjunction with it. Such nails point more or less to physical weakness ; if they are blue, in colour, it is a sure sign of interference with the circulation.

THE CURVED NAIL has somewhat the appearance of the bulbous nail, but it is not as spherical. It shows a nature susceptible to colds and chest troubles.

The colour under the nails should be noted. A white appearance belongs to a cold disposition ; yellowness suggests an excess of bile ; redness, an intense ardour and much strength ; whilst blueness is a clear sign of a poor circulation.

## The Mounts

The Mounts are fleshy domes situated on the palm ; there are seven in all. Four are located at the base of the fingers, two on the side of the hand, on what is termed the percussion, and one at the base of the thumb, which properly constitutes the third phalanx of the thumb. These Mounts are especially valuable in determining the type to which a subject belongs, without which the clearest and most accurate delineation cannot be given.

Each of the fingers is named after the Mount to which it is attached, and partakes of the qualities of its particular Mount. As each Mount represents one of the original types into which the human race was divided, it is only from a due consideration of the development of some one or more of the Mounts that the type of the subject can be obtained.

The first aim in examining the Mounts will be to find which is the strongest one. Whichever it may be, it will show that the qualities of that Mount type are the leading ones. When one Mount is seen large and the others only normal, and of this Mount is a single deep vertical line, while the finger on

the Mount is very long and well developed, it will indicate one who is practically a pure specimen of the type represented by the Mount. In order, however, to judge the extent to which the qualities of this strong Mount will operate, the Mount must not be flabby and its colour should be warm.

It is not often that a hand is seen with only one Mount developed ; sometimes the hand will have two Mounts equally developed, and in such cases there will be a combination of the two types represented by the Mount. To ascertain which is the stronger of these Mounts, if one of them has a deep vertical line on it, or should be harder or redder than the other, this will show it to be the leading Mount.

# The Indications of The Mounts

JUPITER.—Situated at the base of the first or index finger. The Jupiterian is always ambitious and a leader amongst men. He is to be found in all the walks of life. He is to be found in politics, the army, and the church. Religion is a strong feature with the Jupiterian, but he will be found holding all shades of opinion, from the ultra-orthodox to a line close to scepticism—the tip of the finger of Jupiter will tell you to which extreme he leans. Ambition, love of command, pride of position, religion, love of nature, and a love of ceremony and display, are his predominant characteristics. The type is a good and strong one, but a pure Jupiterian is not frequently met with, as there is generally an admixture of other types.

SATURN.—This Mount is situated at the base of the second finger. The Saturnian is a peculiar person, always fastidious and particular even as regards trifles, prudent and wise ; but if the development is excessive, he would be a veritable wet-blanket to damp enthusiasm—his point of view is the gloomy one, and he is ever ready to bring it forward. To bring out its best side, the development should be slight.

He is cynical, devoid of veneration, and ever the doubter. Very unsocial, and does not seek the companionship of others, but is, as a rule, an ardent student, with a liking for chemistry, and is often proficient in occultism. Cautious and prudent, he is very hard to get on with, for he always looks on the dark side of things and is timid and nervous.

He is not one who cares to marry, and in regard to this question very strong indications must be present before

venturing a prediction. Very self-reliant, independent, and cares little for the opinion of others.

APOLLO.—This Mount is situated at the base of the third finger, in conjunction with which it serves to mark out the Apollonian type of individual, and it is one of the pleasantest types to handle.

As a rule, the Apollonian is healthy, happy and genial, strongly artistic, and with him the darker side of life is always in the background. He not only looks to the bright side, but endeavours to make others do so as well, and thus helps to make life worth living.

The Apollonian possesses also a business side, and in this he is often successful, though his love of beauty will probably be displayed in it. Attractive, with a readiness of adaptation to existing conditions and the needs of the public, he lays himself out to attract and please—and success follows.

He is invariably cheerful and happy, but has a quick fierce temper when roused ; he is not one to harbour animosity or resentment, nor is he one to make lasting friendships. He does not therefore inspire lasting friendship in others.

MERCURY.—Found at the base of the fourth finger, this Mount marks an individual of medium height, very compact in build, neat in appearance, and with an expressive countenance, always conveying a sense of restless activity—as a rule he retains a more or less youthful appearance in old age.

He is the most active of all types, both physically and mentally. Proficient in all games and athletic sports, where skill and dexterity rather than physical strength are needed. Possessing as he does good powers of expression, he will be quite at home in debate or argument, and aided by his quick intuition he comes out ahead on his side of the question.

Mercurians are keen in business and shrewd, are excellent actors and mimics, and on the good side they are not vicious, though generally keen and shrewd. They are fond of children and like having them around them, so long as they do not interfere with their other employments. They are versatile and often try a variety of occupations. As a rule, they marry early and are fond of home life.

MARS.—This Mount is of a threefold nature, and consists of the Mount of Mars properly so called, situated under the Mount of Mercury, between the Heart and Head Lines and designated the Upper Mars ; the Lower Mars, situated between the Life line and Mount Venus; and the Plain of Mars,

which constitutes the centre of the plain. Each has its special influence, making this Mount a difficult one to comprehend, while the difficulty is enhanced because there is no finger representing the Mount.

The leading characteristics of the Mount when well developed are courage, self-control, resolution, and capability for command. In almost all hands some Martian development is to be found—to its entire absence is due the flotsam and jetsam of life. Easily discouraged, they go under in the struggle for existence, no matter how gifted or talented they may be.

Given both Mounts well developed, you have one possessed of strong aggressive and resistive powers ; one who will have much persistence, and will resist any attempts to impose on him. Such a subject will push himself over every obstacle, and resist any and every attempt to retard his progress. He will never recognise defeat when it comes.

The Plain of Mars, if well developed, or if crossed with many fine lines, will show the presence of sudden temper.

LUNA.—The qualities of this Mount, situated below Mercury, at the edge of the hand, are to a greater or lesser degree found in nearly all subjects ; but it is not often seen in its fullest development, and its strength must be judged by its curve outwardly, on the percussion of the hand, and the size of the pad it forms on the palm. If it forms a well-defined bulge on the percussion, it must be considered as being *well developed*. If it is also thick, and forms a large pad on the palm, then it must be considered as *very strongly developed* ; while if the bulge is very large, and the pad in the palm equally marked, then the development will be *excessive*.

The Lunarian is often peculiar, especially where the Mount is well developed ; being influenced by the imagination, he becomes dreamy, builds castles in the air, conceives great enterprises of no practical utility. Often imagines he is ill, is fickle, changeable and restless, hence he frequently becomes a great traveller. The more the Mount is lined, the more restless he becomes. He is a great believer in the superstitious, in signs and omens which influence him greatly. He loves music and prefers the classical ; is often a composer, or, if the type is mental, he becomes a writer of fiction or romance, some even of history—but he will be much aided by the possession of a long finger of Mercury, with the first phalanx long, and the qualities of the conic, spatulate or square tip. He is

very fond of the water and makes a good sailor ; he is never generous—is lacking in self-confidence, energy and perseverance and is usually unsuccessful in business.

VENUS.—Found at the base of the thumb, this Mount reveals a healthy, happy, musical and joyous nature. It stands for love, sympathy and generosity. The Venusians are honest and truthful—they are not schemers for money-making and are not given to pettifogging cheating in business. Music always appeals powerfully to them, and wherever a well developed Mount is possessed, there will be found a love of music and particularly of melody. If Mount Luna is equally developed, it will add to the musical taste of the subject.

# The Characteristics of Lines

When examining the Lines of the Hand, the first important point to notice is the character, i.e. their clearness, depth, evenness, whether they are perfect or defective, and if defective, the nature of the defect, how far it extends, and the condition of the Line following the defect.

The first general principal governing the Lines is that the more evenly they run, the clearer they are, the less they are crossed, broken, islanded or chained, and the nearer pink in colour, the better the line is, the more vigorous and clear will be the operation of its attributes. It must be remembered that vertical lines are favourable, while all horizontal lines crossing them are defects—this also applies to the Mounts.

Clear cut, even, pink lines are the best, for every obstruction or defect is inimical.

It must also be noted whether any one line is deeper or shallower than another, is more defective or differs in its character from the other lines in the hand. If the lines, in general, are of the same size and character, but one particular line is much deeper, clearer or better coloured, then the thing which this deep line indicates is the strongest.

If the lines are broad and shallow, they are weak ones, and will show weakness, vacillation and general discouragement. Lines that are deep, well cut in the hand, and well coloured, without being crossed or otherwise defective, show vigour and strength, steadiness of purpose, evenness of temper, and make for general success.

All the changes, obstructions and defects occurring to lines have special names, and these will be considered separately.

THE UNEVEN LINE.—This line may seem clear, but a close examination will show it to be deeper in some parts than in others. In parts, it will be thin, though at other times it may be broad and shallow—these alterations show changes in the character of the line—when deep, strong and vigorous ;

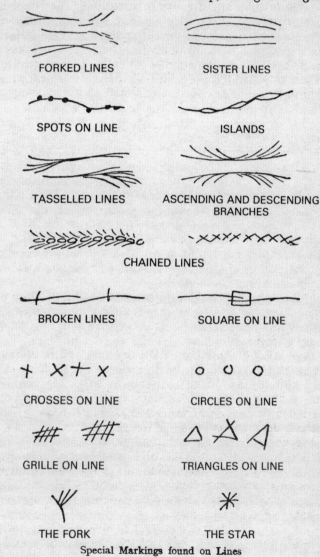

FORKED LINES       SISTER LINES

SPOTS ON LINE       ISLANDS

TASSELLED LINES       ASCENDING AND DESCENDING BRANCHES

CHAINED LINES

BROKEN LINES       SQUARE ON LINE

CROSSES ON LINE       CIRCLES ON LINE

GRILLE ON LINE       TRIANGLES ON LINE

THE FORK       THE STAR

Special Markings found on Lines

when thin, vacillating and weak—thus we get unequal and spasmodic operation of the qualities of this uneven line.

The above indications are applicable to all the lines and not to any particular line.

THE SPLIT LINE.—Fine lines branching from the main lines or Split lines are often seen, and though at times they may run nearly parallel to the line from which they have split, they must not be mistaken for Sister lines as these latter are entirely separate and distinct lines. Nor must they be accounted Islands, as they do not rejoin the line after splitting from it. In general, these Split lines show a weakening of the line during its continuance.

These Split lines are often the beginning of a new course in the life of a subject, in which case the Split line will grow in length. If the Split line only runs a short distance and then stops, it will show that an attempt to change the course of the life has failed. The wider these splits separate from the line, the more important they are, and the more likely to bring about a change in the course of the life. If a Split line runs to a Mount, it shows the attraction of the Mount, and the subject will either follow the qualities of the Mount or will seek the company of subjects of the Mount type.

The Split line will tell of many events, from a mere defect to a total change of life of the subject, and as such they merit close examination.

THE ISLAND.—This sign starts as a Split line, but after running a greater or less distance from the line from which it split, it turns back and rejoins its original line, thus forming a distinct loop to the line. Its size and length varies, but it is always a defect, and the extent of the island indicates the measure of its obstruction or duration, while from the point at which it is seen on the line, the age at which this weakening occurs can be read.

BREAKS are frequently seen, and always indicate a defect, but the kind of break will make a great difference as to its outcome. The wider the break, the more serious it is. Broken lines may be repaired by the broken ends overlapping each other, or by a small cross line uniting them, by sister lines, or by a square enclosing the broken ends. Always a danger, they must be regarded seriously and from their size or the repair signs present, the outcome and effect must be estimated.

THE SQUARE.—This is an individual sign, and with but one exception it is a good sign. No matter how or where the

breaks happen to be, a square repairs or minimises the danger. On occasions, this form is seen on a Mount, in such a position that it does not repair a line. Then, it indicates that any defect of the Mount does not predominate.

The exception, hinted at above, concerns cases where the form is found in the upper portion of the Mount Venus, near to the Life line. In this position, it indicates detention or incarceration.

THE FORK AND TASSEL.—These signs are found at the termination of lines. Some lines fade away until lost in the capillary lines of the skin ; some end abruptly, or with a cross or a dot, star or island, but often they terminate in a Fork or Tassel. These Tassels resemble a number of small short splits at the end of the line, and are often found at the end of a short Life line, Head or Heart line. But wherever found, they indicate the dissipation or gradual diffusion of the qualities of the line and the termination of its usefulness. If a Fork composed of two lines only terminates a line, it amounts to a split, and is not so bad as a Tassel.

THE DOT.—Is not so frequently seen, but is worthy of notice. It needs no explanation as to its appearance, but it varies in size and depth. Dots are always a defect, either on a line or as an independent sign. Small Dots are not serious and often appear after a bad illness, generally of a nervous character. They may be of any colour, and are always subject to repair by a good square.

THE CHAINED LINE.—This gives a line the appearance of being made up of a number of small lines joined together, forming a line which is not clear, even or deep. This tells of a weak operation of the quality of the line it purports to be. If it is the Head line, it will show vacillation, want of self-control, headaches, and other such disturbances. If only a portion of the line is thus chained, then the weakness only extends to the period covered by the defective line.

THE TRIANGLE.—Such a sign is a token of the mental qualities of the possessor. If present at all, it is good, but if very clear, it speaks for decided ability.

THE GRILLE.—This sign is composed of a number of minute lines crossing each other at right angles or nearly so, and is always a serious menace. If very pronounced and composed of deep red lines, the danger is great ; if only made up of small thin lines, it is not so serious. On the Mounts it is a bad sign, bringing up its health defects or its bad qualities.

A Grille composed of lines not running vertical and horizontal is not so serious a defect as one with the lines running more nearly at right angles.

CROSS-BARS.—These are constituted of horizontal lines lying close together, but without vertical lines crossing them. This sign will bring out the worst side of a Mount, such as health defects, but fortunately it is not often seen. The deeper the lines composing it, the worse will be the indication.

THE CIRCLE is a very unusual sign, and is chiefly valuable when seen on the Life line or the Mount of Apollo—or the Line of Head under Apollo. Such a marking will tell of *delicacy* of the eyes. It is not found on the hands of *all* blind persons, but chiefly on the hands of those who have poor vision or weak eyes.

THE TRIDENT, or three-pronged spear-head, is found at the upper end of the line. It is a favourable indication, and adds strength to the Line of Apollo, increasing its brilliancy and the chances of success. It is a very unusual marking and is always a good one. It must, however, be perfectly marked to ensure its fullest indication.

THE STAR is an important and valuable sign ; it is sometimes a good indication, but at other times a bad one according to its location. Whenever seen on the hand, it should be regarded as of the utmost importance. If small and evenly formed in all its proportions, it will mean brightness or intensification ; but if large, ill-formed and diffused, it indicates a break-up or an abrupt ending.

THE CROSS is a very usual sign to be seen, though it appears sometimes as a single sign, or is formed by lines crossing other lines. Always note the depth of the lines forming it and how they conform in proportion to the other lines. A deep cut, highly coloured cross is of great import. The Cross is an obstacle or defect, or a change in the course of the subject's life. In any position it must be regarded as an unfavourable sign.

# The Lines of the Hand

A chart of the hand is shown on p. 131. All the usual lines figure on it ; but it must not be expected that every hand will bear a complete set of them ; in fact, such a hand would be rare.

Taking the lines separately, we will commence with the line affecting the heart.

THE HEART LINE arises from some point under or near the finger of Jupiter, and then traces its course across the upper portion of the palm, under the Mounts, terminating

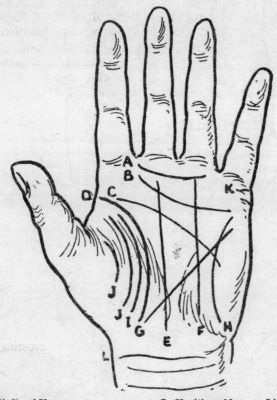

A. Girdle of Venus
B. Heart Line
C. Head Line
D. Life Line
E. Fate or Saturn Line
F. Success or Apollo Line
G. Health or Mercury Line
H. Intuition Line
I. Mars Line
JJ. Influence Lines
K. Affection Lines
L. Rascettes or Bracelets

on the percussion. It is of primary importance, as it deals with the mechanism which controls the life stream, and which so largely influences the health and temperament.

The general rule is that if the line is single and clear, the

possessor will be noted for his kindly nature and his thought for others. The deeper and clearer the line at its start, the deeper are the affections, but they are likely to be tinged with selfishness. The more the line branches, the more the affections will go out to others.

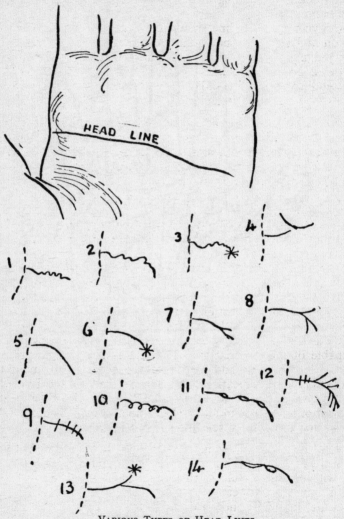

VARIOUS TYPES OF HEAD LINES
Chained Lines are shown at 1, 2, 10, etc. Stars at 3, 6, and 13.
Islands at 11 and 14. Cross-bars at 9 and 12

THE HEAD LINE should start out from the Life line, to which, normally, it is slightly attached, before it branches away across the Plain of Mars. Its course should be in a somewhat sloping direction towards the percussion, either falling to Mount Luna or running in a more or less straight route across the hand.

In every case the line should be of a good length, even in depth and clearness, not broken or otherwise defective—then the judgment will be good, the head sound, the sense strong, with good intellectual faculties. A broken, defective, descending or pale line indicates weakness, headaches, want of fixity of ideas, and irresolution.

THE LIFE LINE rises at the side of the hand, well under the finger of Jupiter ; encircling the Mounts of Lower Mars and Venus, it terminates in most cases under Mount Venus. The line should be well cut, clear of defects, not broad and shallow, and continuous ; not too red in colour, nor too pale, but rather pink. The colour tests are peculiarly applicable to it.

The line indicates the health of the subject during the various periods of life, and also whether the course of the life is upwards or downwards, and in many instances it shows the probable termination of life.

This line is rarely absent ; indeed, its total absence would show that the subject was extremely precarious, and that death might come at any moment.

As a general proposition, the longer the Life line, the longer will be the life, and the shorter the line the shorter the life. Experience, however, shows that this general proposition is capable of much variation. The fact is the Life line shows the *natural* vigour and health of the subject. It must be remembered that death is not shown alone on the Life line —the lines of the Head, Heart, and Mercury also show death indications. Hence in all cases of importance, it is absolutely necessary to compare the line in both hands.

THE FATE LINE, sometimes called the Line of Saturn, indicates the natural kind of career of the subject, and whether it will be successful, settled, or varying and changeable. It is not often absent, but when this happens, it does not indicate a purely negative existence. " In the course of my career," says Psychos, the celebrated palmist, " I have met several successful business men in whose hands the line was absent ; I found them glorying in the fact that they were

' self-made men,' and by their own energy they had surmounted the handicap of the absent line."

There is no regular starting point for this line—it starts from many places, and not always even at the base of the

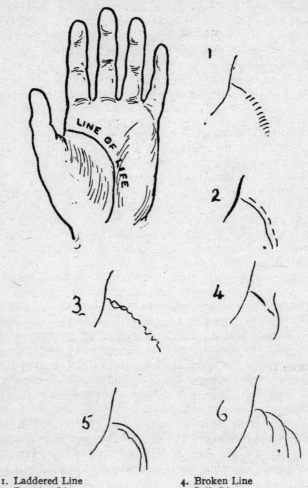

1. Laddered Line
2. Doubled Line
3. Chained Line
4. Broken Line
5. Split Line
6. Wavy Line

hand. But start where it may, it always runs towards the Mount of Saturn. It will sometimes be found rising from the *inside* of the Life line; then, if it runs to the Mount of

Saturn, it will tell not only of material success in life, but that near relatives will afford assistance. If it takes its rise from Mount Luna, and runs to the Mount of Saturn, then success will be attained, but one of the opposite sex will largely assist—this aid may be given either by advice and suggestion, or money. Rising from the centre of the palm and running to its Mount, the subject will attain success chiefly by his own efforts and will, in fact, be the architect of his own fortunes.

This line is subject to variations as to its *Character*, for unless it is as deep as the other lines in the hand, the indications of the line will be out of their proper proportions, and it will not operate so well as if it balanced with the other lines. If it is very deep and well-cut, the subject will possess good capabilities, the right use of which will undoubtedly bring success. If this deep line extends to the Mount, then the favourable conditions will continue during the life.

If the line, however, should be short, the good conditions will be present only during the length of the line. The line being *Thin* will show that though there are natural advantages present, great exertion will be needed for their full development.

THE SUCCESS LINE, often spoken of as the Line of Apollo, has no fixed starting point, nor is it to be found on all hands ; but wherever found, it will run toward the Mount of Apollo. It may rise from various points of the hand, such as the Line of Life, the Mount of Luna or the Plain of Mars, sometimes terminating high up on the Mount, and sometimes not reaching the Mount. Whenever it is present, it emphasizes the Apollonian traits and qualifications, and indicates a capability or possibility of accomplishing a good deal. Without this line, the prospects of rising to fame, however clever or talented, are more or less remote.

The length of the line determines the extent and duration of its influence—the longer the line the more effect it will have, while the shorter the line the less will be its importance. A Line of Apollo, starting from the wrist, running through the hand and reaching the Mount, will indicate the possession of great talent. If the line starts low in the hand, and runs only for a short distance, the subject possesses talents, but they will not be productive of great results.

If the line rises higher in the hand, and covers the space between the Head and Heart lines (*i.e.* the Quadrangle),

the special talents of the subject will operate during that period. If the line runs on to the Mount, he will be well endued with Apollonian characteristics, and in whichever world he moves will be brilliant and acquire reputation.

THE HEALTH or MERCURY LINE should start on Mount Luna and run upwards, on the percussion of the hand, to the Mount of Mercury, from which Mount it derives its name. It is a valuable line, as it affords an indication of the condition of the digestive organs, and in conjunction with the Line of Life, Saturn and Apollo, it is especially important as a guide to business success, owing to its health indications.

Although this line should rise from Mount Luna, I have found in my own practice that it rarely does so. In the majority of hands, it will be found rising from towards the Lines of Saturn or Life, sometimes from the base or centre of the hand, and often in the plane of Mars. When rising from the Line of Life, it tells but too surely of heart weakness —not necessarily disease. This marking should be of peculiar interest to the medical profession, as it reveals tendencies that the stethoscope may fail to disclose.

To afford the best promise of success, this line should not at any point in its course touch the Line of Life. The source of the line, either outside and apart from the Line of Life, is immaterial.

The presence of a really good, clear, deep-cut and well coloured line is rarely seen, especially after the subject has passed the stage of youth. In many hands, the line may be entirely absent ; this indicates a person who, other things being equal, will be vivacious, quick in manner and speech, not knowing anything of liver trouble, and to whom life is indeed worth living.

The character of the line is of primary importance, as a deep and clear line of Mercury not only indicates a good constitution and strong vitality, but also a clear brain and a good memory. A good Head line will be much disturbed, and its operations impeded, by a poor line of Mercury.

THE GIRDLE OF VENUS—As a rule, this line rises between the fingers of Jupiter and Saturn, and runs in a semi-circle under the Mounts of Saturn and Apollo, ending between the fingers of Apollo and Mercury. It may also take its rise on the Mount of Jupiter, ending on Mount Mercury, or even at times extending to the percussion. It is, in part, a sister line

to the Heart line, and in some cases when the Heart line is absent it takes its place.

This line is a subject of much misconception ; many palmists regard it as a menace to the morality of its possessor, but its presence does not as a rule indicate immorality or licentiousness, but that in the majority of cases it indicates a highly sensitive and nervous subject. If the hand is a weak one, expect hysteria.

It is by no means an uncommon sign, being seen frequently in hands of all types. In many instances of hands which contain the Girdle, the palm will be crossed by many fine lines, running in all directions, which in itself is an added confirmation of an intensely nervous temperament.

THE LINE OF INTUITION, when present, lies on the side of the hand near the percussion. It rises on Mount Luna, curves inwards towards the palm, and ends on or near Mount Mercury. Its position is near the line of Mercury, but its distinguishing feature lies in its decided curve.

The presence of this line, if well and clearly marked, adds greatly to the intuitive faculties, and tends to increase the Mercurian keenness. Its possessors receive impressions for which they cannot account, and are given to form opinions which are accurate, though they are quite unable to give any reasons for such opinions. I have found it result in increased sensitiveness and added keenness in estimating the characters of people. Many are not conscious of the possession of such faculties, but with this marking they *feel* things, though why they do so they are quite at a loss to say.

In judging the effect or power of this line, regard must be had to the character of the hand in which it is found. In a hand which is hard, with square fingers and tips, and with but few lines on it, the intuition afforded by the line will be passed over as foolish. But with long fingers, pointed tips, Mount Luna full, the Head line sloping, the subject will be strongly psychic and will dream dreams, have visions, strong presentiments of danger—in fact, the subject is one before whom coming events will cast their shadows, and they will be strong believers in signs and omens. This sign or line I have often seen in the hands of clairvoyants and Spiritualist mediums.

A deep, clear line will give the greatest amount of intuition, whilst if broken or otherwise defective it will limit its effectiveness. An Island on the line will indicate that the intuitiveness resulting from the line will bring little success.

THE LINE OF MARS.—This is a line which rises on the Lower Mount of Mars, and runs very close to but inside the line of Life. It is, in fact, a sister line to it, and must lie very close to it. Its presence in the hand assures a stronger constitution to its possessor than even that indicated by a deep, clear and well-cut line of Life. But it must be considered in connection with the line of Life and the type of the subject. Should the line of Life be marked by defects, with the line of Mars present, the person will be subject to delicacy, but there will be an underlying strength which will operate to prevent serious trouble being experienced. This added vitality will, if the line extends the full length of the line of Life, continue throughout the life ; but if only existing during a portion of the line of Life, its influence will be marked for the period indicated.

Lines rising from the line of Mars, if crossing the line of Life, indicate a tendency to rise in life, due to increased physical ardour. If such a rising line reaches to and merges into the line of Head, it will occasion increased mental force as an additional aid to success—a similar result will accrue should such rising line merge in the line of Saturn.

It is essential, with this line present, to note carefully the type of the subject and the general character of the hand, for if the hand is sensual, the line of Life strong, deep and clear, with Mount Venus large, then (with the line of Mars clear) you will have one who will be prone to excessive indulgence of the sexual appetites, which will need an unusually deep and clear line of Head and a strong Thumb to restrain. With such a hand, if a line from the line of Mars runs to and cuts the line of Apollo, or the line of Saturn, it will indicate that such excessive indulgence has interfered with the career. If the line of Apollo terminates in a Dot, Bar or Cross, then the subject will also suffer a loss of reputation. If such rising line, in such a hand, cuts a line of affection, then the domestic life of the subject will be ruined by excess.

THE LINES OF MARRIAGE.—On some hands, a number of these lines are to be found : others reveal none. When present, they may be seen running from the edge of the palm towards the centre.

They are frequently met on the hands of people who have never married ; hence, it is more correct to call them lines of Affection.

If many lines of Affection are seen on the hand, it will indicate that the subject is very susceptible in affairs of the

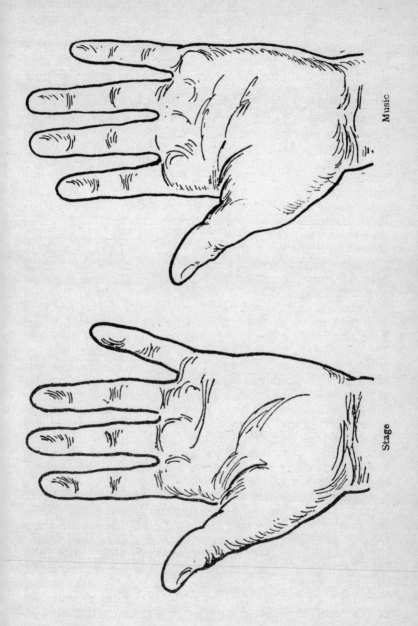

Music

Stage

heart—in fact, very much of a flirt. In such cases, the strength
of the affection will be indicated by the strength or weakness
of the lines.

When the lines of Affection are thinner than the other
lines in the hand, it will indicate that the subjects have no
really strong affection and are undemonstrative in their
affections. Should the line start deep and strong and then
grow thin and weak, the affection will weaken.

These lines, as in the case with the other lines in the hand,
are subject to obstacles. Thus, a Cross on a line of Affection
will indicate a serious obstacle to the affections, while a Star
will tell of a total breach. A Break will show an interference
in the course of the affection ; a Fork at the end of the line
will tell of separation, and, with other indications, of divorce.

A branch or turning of the line of Affection towards the
Heart line, will indicate the death of the person beloved, and
often from the point where the line of Affection touches the
Heart line, a fine line will run to a point in the Life line, which
will indicate the date when such an event will happen. Drooping
branches from the line of Affection will indicate much sorrow
and disappointment in married life.

Too much care cannot be taken in dealing with these lines
of Affection ; it is essential to take into consideration the
indications of marriage to be found in other parts of the hand.
The lines of Life and Saturn will generally afford a more
reliable ground for predicting marriage. Often the Life line
will show a break and a change in the line, when the character
of the line after the break will show whether such change has
been or will be beneficial or otherwise. In addition, it frequently occurs that a new line of influence starts from such a
break and runs inside the Life line and close to it. If such an
influence line, after running for a space close to the Life line,
widens out from it, it will tell of a want of sympathy or close-
ness on the part of the influence.

As regards the indications of marriage on the line of
Saturn, they will be found in lines from Mount Luna joining
the line of Saturn, which invariably indicate an influence
joining the life—the subsequent character of the line of Saturn
will show the purpose of the influence on the life. Lines from
Mount Luna coming to, but not joining, the line of Saturn will
be but transient influences—but should the line cross the
line of Saturn, it will tell of an influence crossing the life. If
at the point of crossing, a hollow is shown on the hand, a

disappointment will have been experienced; following this hollow, the line of Saturn will often be defective for a period.

SIGNS OF WIDOWHOOD.—A break in the line of Affection indicates the sudden death of the partner; when the line of Affection, after going straight for a time and without breaking, turns down to and touches the Heart line; when the line of Affection is cut at its termination by another line; by the line of Affection terminating in a Star on Mount Mercury. As to whether these signs relate to a past or future event, the age at which the event is noted should be ascertained, while the lines of Life, Heart, and Saturn should be examined for indications of change or shock at the age corresponding with that of the sign on the marriage line.

THE RASCETTES or BRACELETS are the lines which cross the wrist. In many hands, they are three in number, but in others there may be only two, or even one.

The first Rascette, if deep and clear, will add confirmation to the other indications in the hand of the possession of a strong constitution : doubtless it will add strength to a long, clear and deep Life line. Should, however, the Rascette be poorly marked, be broad and shallow or chained, the constitution will be weak.

Long branches from the Rascette, rising high into the Mount of Luna, are known as travel lines, and are read to indicate voyages : should such a line run to the Mount of Jupiter, the voyage will be a long and happy one.

A straight line from the Rascette to the Mount of Mercury indicates a sudden and unexpected increase in the finances : a similar line rising to and joining the line of Saturn will indicate the return of a friend from across the water.

THE LINES OF INFLUENCE are only of importance in so much as they add strength to whatever reading is derived from the Line of Mars.

# EVERYBODY'S BIRTHDAY GUIDE

## WHEN WERE YOU BORN?

YOUR CHARACTERISTICS, CAREER, HEALTH,
MARRIAGE FATE, AND LUCKY SIGNS

## SHOW THIS TO YOUR FRIENDS

The Zodiac is a circular belt in the sky through which the Sun, Moon and the chief planets trace their regular paths. Thousands of years ago, the astrologers divided this belt into twelve more or less regular portions and gave to each an appropriate name and sign; the latter, we know as the Signs of the Zodiac.

It requires no great amount of imagination to recognise that, when the Sun enters one of these twelve heavenly divisions, it influences everything that comes under its sway. It may be for good and it may be for bad; it depends entirely on the conditions and the circumstances.

Long years of careful watching and noting have enabled the astrologers to glean some of the influences of the Sun upon the Zodiacal divisions, and those which refer to the characteristics and fates of average normal individuals are set out in these pages.

It must be pointed out that, since the present calendar has been observed, the twelve months do not correspond with the twelve Zodiacal divisions. As a rule, the Zodiacal periods commence on the 19th to 22nd of a month and terminate on a similar date in the following month. Thus *Capricorn* begins on December 22nd and ends on January 20th. *Aquarius* opens on January 21st and, in its turn, closes on February 19th. The others follow in rotation, until December comes round once more and *Capricorn* is again in evidence.

It may be of interest to add that the first of the signs is *Pisces* and the last, *Aquarius ;* thus the Zodiacal New Year falls late in March.

# Were You Born between December 22nd and January 20th?

## The Period of Capricorn

Capricorn rules the period between December 22nd and January 20th. It has a goat, possessing the tail of a fish for its sign. Saturn is the planet which guides its destinies.

GENERAL CHARACTERISTICS.—If you were born under the sway of this sign, you are a very practical person and equally capable. You are very tidy by nature, you love order and are methodical. It is even possible that these qualities are too highly developed in you, and it may be that, while attending to minute details, you lose some of the larger opportunities of life.

You are sensitive and generous and there is much sympathy in your " make-up." Were you to hear of a case of want or somebody in dire distress, it is unthinkable that you would pass by and not hold out a helping hand.

In one direction you do not excel. Though you have the qualities for making your way in the world and it is within your powers to climb high up the ladder of success, you are apt to hesitate. This is due to a curious reticence in your nature which does not allow you to thrust yourself forward. You wonder whether you have the necessary qualities to carry you through and, while you are wondering, some more pushing but less well-equipped person steps into your place. Therefore, do not think so much of your mythical limitations ; take it for granted that you will succeed and you will. This applies to women just as much as to men.

OCCUPATIONS.—Being methodical and careful about details, you are well-fitted for such work as is afforded by the Civil Service. You would do well in a bank and, in many respects, you have the painstaking qualities required for the scholastic profession. In businesses, where success depends on rigid routine, you ought to be happy, and all the posts which fall to people who can plod their way through examinations should be within your grasp.

This desire for method and order is reflected in the homes of Capricorn women. Whether a large house or two small rooms are concerned, the place will be tidy, everything will be where it should be, and the time-table of the home will be run as though by clockwork. This attention to tidiness and punctuality may be carried even to excess. Such little trivialities as cigarette-ash dropped on the carpet or a tardy arrival for dinner may cause more bother than they are worth. But this must not be taken to infer that the Capricorn woman is a fault-finder at heart. She is certainly not ; she will worry, however, over small details that run counter to her orderly and methodical nature.

From all this, you will see that you are practical, methodical and generous ; but that you are apt to think too much of small details and that you do not place sufficient faith in your own capabilities.

HOBBIES AND PASTIMES.—Regarding hobbies and pastimes, you will find that those which appeal to you most will be of a character which call for brains rather than muscle. At them you will succeed well enough.

LOVE MATTERS.—In matters of love, the Capricorn men and women are, generally, very careful in taking a partner. The horror of making a possible mistake seems to be magnified in their eyes and they are very cautious. As a consequence, they marry later than usual ; but, once they do make a choice, they become charming and devoted husbands and wives, especially when their partners were born under the sway of Taurus or Scorpio.

In one particular, the Capricorn woman is highly fortunate. Should she marry above her station, she has the facility for raising herself to the level of her husband and hiding her lowly origin.

DATES.—You will find, during certain periods of the year, that you are able to achieve everything you desire and, at other times, things habitually take on an adverse complexion. This is only to be expected, once the Zodiacal influence on the World is appreciated. Your best periods are during Taurus and Scorpio, and your worst while Aries is passing. Therefore, let all your new and important ventures take shape in the good intervals and see to it that Aries is a period for marking time.

LIFE, HEALTH, ETC.—The length of your life depends more on yourself than on the Fates. You have the power to attain a ripe old age ; but, if you wish to do so, you must take

particular care of your lungs. Seek all the fresh air you can obtain and, without making yourself a faddist, dwell as much as possible under the sky of heaven. Make a practice of regular walking and see that your head is up and your chest open. Colds and coughs should never be neglected, and damp air is highly injurious.

As a secondary caution, look to your digestion. Never overload it with foods that are rich and hard to digest. Plain food will serve you best.

Capricorn children are often delicate until they are about seven years of age. If carefully tended until then, there is every likelihood that a great change for the better will be manifested at that age. Thereafter they are robust, if due caution is observed.

LUCKY PORTENTS.—Capricorn people derive good luck from these colours : black and dark brown.

Their mascot should be the garnet.

Their lucky day of the week is Saturday.

Their luck will be enhanced if they consider lead as their fortunate metal.

# Were You Born between January 21st and February 19th?

## The Period of Aquarius

Aquarius rules the period between January 21st and February 19th. It is symbolised by a man pouring out a stream of water from a pitcher on to Pisces, the fishes. Uranus is the planet which chiefly guides its destinies.

GENERAL CHARACTERISTICS.—If you were born under the sway of this sign, you are a person of considerable action. You are never still ; you are always making plans and the thing you can tolerate least is inactivity. You have much self-will, and the spirit of independence is firmly planted in you. You resent the interference of others, perhaps more than you should, and freedom is a quality you prize very highly—freedom not only of action but also of thought.

Since you possess the two qualities of activity and of making plans, it follows that you will think out things that are original in character. These may take widely diverse forms. You might invent some very ingenious contrivance or evolve a

new method of marketing goods. Whatever it is, the world will be taken a step forward on your account.

There is no doubt that you set great store on honesty, using the term in its widest sense, and you require your friends to be honest in purpose and honest in speech, as well as in money affairs.

So much for your good points, which are certainly plentiful. Your greatest weakness lies in the way you treat your fellow creatures. You cannot tolerate inefficiency and you are apt to consider those who do not see " eye to eye " with you as being hopelessly beneath contempt. It would not be difficult for you to cultivate a more charitable and tolerant view towards those who are likely to earn your disapproval. At any rate, it is well worth trying.

OCCUPATIONS.—There are many remunerative occupations which might engage your energies profitably. Your aptitude for making plans fits you for a whole host of businesses and trades where originality counts—and this applies just as much to women as to men. Trained in another direction, the same quality would help in organising ; thus you are eminently fitted for directing the details of large commercial concerns. What you should avoid are all those jobs which are the same year in, year out, and where one day's work is merely a repetition of another. Routine jobs are not for you.

As far as women's housework is concerned, the position is somewhat contradictory. An Aquarian housewife will chafe at the daily duties which recur seven days a week ; but she will delight in re-arranging the contents of a room or in being the hostess at her own dinner-table, because these are things that call for planning and which are not repeated often enough to be boring.

HOBBIES AND PASTIMES.—Travel is the pastime which appeals to you most, had you the leisure and the money to indulge in it wholeheartedly. As it is, you may have to content yourself with lesser diversions. Card-playing is welcomed and there is no doubt that you are able to derive a good deal of pleasure by making things—it may be anything from a wireless set to a batch of photographic prints.

LOVE MATTERS.—Aquarians drift into matrimony almost as a matter of course. Very frequently, there is no courtship, so much as a friendship. This is especially noticeable when both parties were born in this particular period.

An Aquarian lover is not demonstrative. He or she will refrain from penning ardent letters of affection and the less romance that comes into the affair the better. But do not conclude that he or she views marriage in a detached light. Far from it. An Aquarian who marries does so with the full intention of making the union as harmonious as is humanly possible, and this ideal is not cast aside after the lapse of a few years.

DATES.—You will find, during certain periods of the year, that you are able to achieve everything you desire and, at other times, things habitually take on an adverse complexion. Your best periods are during Gemini and Libra, and your worst while Taurus is passing. On this account, you should be active in undertaking new and important projects in the good intervals and cautious during Taurus.

LIFE, HEALTH, ETC.—From the point of view of health, you are fortunate. You have an excellent constitution ; but if any part of your body is less robust than the rest, it is your heart and all that immediately depends on it. Therefore, consider yourself carefully when the age of forty is reached and avoid overstrain.

As a secondary caution, avoid damaging your eyes. This, however, applies more to early youth than to later life. If you have passed this age and your sight is unimpaired, you may reckon that the danger no longer exists.

Stimulants have a specially bad effect on Aquarians and, if these are shunned ruthlessly, there is every reason to suppose that you will attain a good age and live a long, useful life.

LUCKY PORTENTS.—Aquarian people derive good luck from these colours : black and blue.

Their mascot should be the amethyst.

Their lucky day of the week is Monday.

There is luck for them in coal.

# Were You Born between February 20th and March 20th ?

## The Period of Pisces

Pisces rules the period between February 20th and March 20th. It is symbolised by a pair of fishes. Jupiter is the planet which guides its destinies.

GENERAL CHARACTERISTICS.—If you were born under the sway of this sign, your outstanding character is that of sympathy, mingled with hospitality. You have a great urge to make your fellow-creatures a little happier for having met you. No higher quality could be possessed than this ; but it is one that may be carried to excess. Pisceans have been known to spend time and money they could ill afford on alleviating the wants of others.

Your tastes are of a cultured order and, at heart, you have a love for literary and artistic works of a high grade, though the commercial existence, which you must probably follow, may force them out of sight. Coupled with these qualities, you have a vivid imagination which leads you to " build castles in the air " on occasion.

Regarding money, you have peculiar views. At times you deny yourself legitimate necessaries and, at others, you spend somewhat recklessly. You will always give in response to the call of charity ; but, on occasion, you will put yourself to considerable trouble in order to save a few coppers on the price of an article you desire to purchase.

Your chief weakness, however, is that you are somewhat easily impressed ; in fact, you are apt to believe too much of what you hear. Unscrupulous people are quick to notice this defect in your " make-up " and they are certain to trade on it sooner or later. Therefore, be on your guard and avoid being victimised by someone who may come to you in the guise of a friend.

OCCUPATIONS.—Your desire for benefiting mankind and alleviating sufferings will find ample scope in the medical profession or in nursing, should you be a woman. In either of these, you would be able to live up to your ambitions and do really good and useful work in the world. Failing the possibility of entering these professions, there are still opportunities that will agree with your temperament. As a teacher in a poor neighbourhood, you could perform really excellent service. You would fulfil the duties of a manager or supervisor of a large staff with courage and kindness, and people would submit to your orders willingly, knowing that they could always count on you as a friend.

In quite another field you may safely rely on earning a good living. It is in the literary and journalistic world. You have imagination as well as literary and artistic expression, and these single you out for an author's life. If you take up

a post of this character, it would not be surprising to find that your spare time was spent, voluntarily, in furthering some humanitarian work, especially if you are an unmarried woman.

Men of Pisces are fond of the sea and we find them filling their duties cheerfully, from captains down to the lowest deck hands. When they take on this life, they usually become thoroughly enamoured with it and never want to leave it.

Women of Pisces are very enthusiastic about managing their homes, but only if there are children there. A home without children is, to them, no home at all.

HOBBIES AND PASTIMES.—Reading, painting, the drama, and such pastimes as require artistic and literary feeling will occupy your mind. It would not be surprising to find that you suddenly developed an interest in Spiritualism or things relating to the supernatural. Anything to do with travel will also attract you, whether it is on land, sea or in the air. For such games as cricket and football, you will have very little time.

LOVE MATTERS.—Pisceans, from their very nature, require friendship and love, in order to exist. Therefore, they marry early, though they generally have more than one love-affair before making a binding choice. When married, they are admirable partners ; but it has been noticed that two Pisceans do not form the best union. Thus, a person born during the period of Pisces is not advised to choose a partner of the same sign. Those of the Pisces period are best mated with those of Scorpio or Cancer.

DATES.—You will find, during certain periods of the year that you are able to achieve everything you attempt, whilst, at other times, you are much less successful in your fortunes. If you take the trouble to work out these periods, you will find that it is during the sway of Gemini, Cancer and Libra that you are fortunate, and during Scorpio that ill-fortune dogs your footsteps. Therefore, let all your new and important ventures take shape in the former periods and see to it that the latter is one for marking time.

LIFE, HEALTH, ETC.—There is nothing to cause worry, regarding matters of health. While you cannot claim a perfect constitution, there is no great flaw in it ; but you must take care. Pisceans are not the strongest, yet those who have studied their health and taken note of warnings, in time, have lived to a good age. The lungs are usually the weakest

spot, but the nerves may give trouble, too. Live, as far as possible, a natural life ; get out in the fresh air whenever you can, and be temperate in your food and drink.

LUCKY PORTENTS.—People of the Piscean period derive good luck from the colours, blue, purple and mauve.

Their mascot should be the bloodstone.

Their lucky day of the week is Saturday.

There is no special metal to aid their fortunes.

# Were You Born between March 21st and April 19th?

## The Period of Aries

Aries rules the period between March 21st and April 19th. It is symbolised by a ram, possessing horns that are formidable. Mars is the planet which guides its destinies.

GENERAL CHARACTERISTICS.—If you were born under the sway of this sign you are an energetic person, never satisfied unless you are " up and doing." Should you be typical of your type you are strong in mind and strong in body, and are full of enthusiasm for the work in hand. You have unlimited courage, and all these qualities combined tend to make your life varied. You are not going to stay at one thing just because you have set out in that direction. You will change your job, your friends, your hobbies, or any plans whatsoever, if you think the change is for the better. Unfortunately for you, you will not always count up the " pros and cons " of the change as carefully as you should, and this impulsiveness may often lead you into difficulties. Still, you have courage, you are a born fighter, and are endowed with plenty of enterprise ; all of which will enable you to succeed in the end.

It is unlikely that you will amass great wealth ; but money is only useful for the happiness it can bring and of happiness you will have your full share and more.

There are many reasons for thinking that you will move from place to place a good deal and, probably, you will see much of the world. If a man, you are likely to take up posts in various parts of the Empire and, if a woman, it would not be surprising were you called upon to travel because of the requirements of your husband's business or profession.

If a word or two of caution may be offered, we would suggest that you should endeavour to cultivate the quality of patience, and that you reason out the cost more thoroughly before embarking upon some fresh enterprise. These are little points, but they help to mar your success. Moreover, avoid being a " rolling-stone," especially after the age of thirty (women) and thirty-five (men).

OCCUPATIONS.—You will not be happy in any occupation that is humdrum and safe. As long as every day brings its fresh set of problems to be solved and surmounted, you will be satisfied ; but anything with a spice of danger or intrepidity in it will please you even more. Translating these general remarks into concrete examples, we assert that the profession of a surgeon would appeal to you, because people's lives and your own reputation depend upon your actions. At the other end of the scale is the work of a constructional engineer who has to overcome exceptional difficulties in building, say, a mighty bridge. This, again, would appeal to you, not because the two are alike in practice, but because they entail the same fundamental qualities.

In the case of women, it has been noticed that they possess some curious ability for managing any work that calls for the use of fire or heat. Thus, they are good cooks ; but this is only one of a hundred occupations that might be mentioned.

HOBBIES AND PASTIMES.—People of Aries are exceptionally good with their hands. The men can make things for the home and the women are expert needle workers, painters, cooks, etc. The Ariean father takes a delight in mending his youngsters' toys and the Ariean mother prefers to make the children's clothes, rather than buy them. The Ariean boy and girl fusses with gold-fish, pet tortoises or canaries in cages.

LOVE MATTERS.—Love comes early in life to the Ariean and, when it comes, it strikes a very ardent note. But big flames die out quickly and the Ariean is in and out of love many times before the final choice is made. Probably, the wedding will not be an early one ; nevertheless, it will be a happy one as long as two Arieans do not mate together. They are too much alike to be perfectly happy with each other. The best partners for the Arieans are those born during the passage of Scorpio or Sagittarius.

DATES.—During certain periods of the year, you will notice that you are able to achieve everything you attempt whilst at other times you are much less successful in your

efforts. Should you make it your business to look into these periods, you will find that it is during the sway of Cancer and Leo that you are fortunate and during Taurus that ill-fortune attends you. Therefore, let all your new and important ventures take shape in the good periods and see to it that Taurus is a period for avoiding troubles.

LIFE, HEALTH, ETC.—Your health need not cause you any worry, but it must not be neglected. Your chief danger lies in submitting yourself to excesses of heat and cold, particularly the former. Either are bad for you. Beware of sunstroke especially if you have to travel in the Tropics, and avoid everything that might tend to send up your temperature. Apoplexy, in later life, must be guarded against.

It is highly important that you get plenty of sleep and do not keep late hours. This is imperative because, in your waking hours, you are excessively energetic and never still—all of which use up your vitality very rapidly. It is only with the aid of ample sleep that the loss can be repaired.

LUCKY PORTENTS.—Ariean people derive good luck from the colour scarlet, though all shades of red tend to fortunate conditions.

Their mascot should be the diamond.

Their lucky day of the week is Thursday.

The metal which will bring them most luck is iron.

# Were You Born between April 20th and May 20th?

## The Period of Taurus

Taurus rules the period between April 20th and May 20th. It is symbolised by a mighty bull. Venus is the planet which guides its destinies.

GENERAL CHARACTERISTICS.—If you were born under the sway of this sign you are a person who places comfort and happiness before everything else. This, however, must not be taken to mean that you will neglect your duties for the sake of these requirements. Quite the reverse ; you will work and strive, knowing that it is only by industry that you will be able to attain them satisfactorily.

You have the " herd instinct": that is to say you like

company and are not happy when alone. Consequently, you will seek out friendships and value them.

There is every reason to suppose that that typical British gentleman, John Bull, was a Taurian. You and he have many traits in common, not necessarily in appearances, nor even in sex ; but you both love truth and vigour ; you are both capable ; you both admire efficiency, and it takes a great deal to make you rise up and rend your adversary. Both of you, again, are shrewd in financial matters. John is the banker of the world and you are a sound banker of your own personal fortunes.

The worst that can be said of you is that you applaud what is old and well-tried and do not give new things a fair trial. As a result, you are apt to stick in a rut and stay there. If you are over fifty, it is more than likely that you have a poor opinion of the rising generation, that you decry their modernistic views and behaviour and, generally, rate them at a lower value than you should.

Taurian women are remarkably good-hearted and they are noted for their love of children. Their own offspring come in for a good deal of petting and are often spoilt in consequence.

OCCUPATIONS.—Almost any work that requires steady, intelligent plodding will give you satisfaction, especially in middle life or later. Your judgment is sound and you are thorough in all you do ; but you do not care for work that must be done in fits and starts. You want to be left in peace and quiet to get on with your duties. You resent being hurried.

Your methodical nature fits you for being placed in authority over others and, as you are placid and not fiery-tempered, you will secure the loyalty of those you have to direct.

You possess a head for finance, which suggests that you would do well in the banking world, in the office of a financier or a stock-broker ; but most office work would suit your temperament.

Should you be a woman, you could admirably perform the duties of a typist, a housekeeper, a cook or a teacher, as long as those placed in authority over you were not of the worrying type.

HOBBIES AND PASTIMES.—You set rather a high value on your leisure and begrudge losing any part of it when a rush of work comes along. Your aim is to spend as much time as possible in the open air, which is, of course, highly wise of you.

You are not a lover of strenuous games ; but such pastimes

as walking, rowing, fishing and nature study are more in keeping with your ideals.

LOVE MATTERS.—You are sociable and look upon a wide circle of friends as the correct state for happiness. From among these friends, you will single out one who means everything to you and that one you will marry, if you have not already done so.

Your nature is full of sympathy. Consequently, there is every reason for affirming that your married life will be a happy one. You are the sort that thinks a great deal of your home and its contents, and you expect it to be a comfortable, well-kept place. Disorder in the house is likely to grate on your susceptibilities.

Your children will mean a great deal to you. You will slave for them and give them the utmost in education and enjoyment, and what you lavish on them will not be wasted. Your partner will act in greatest harmony with you if born during the rule of Leo, Virgo or Sagittarius.

DATES.—During certain periods of the year, namely those of Gemini, Cancer and Sagittarius, you will find that all you undertake is attended with good fortune; while during the sway of Scorpio and Libra things are not nearly so propitious. You must mark out these periods, using the former for all your most important ventures and, during the latter, it will be well to take things cautiously.

LIFE, HEALTH, ETC.—You have already been told that you put a high price on your comforts. As an outcome of this trait, you are something of a " gourmet " and enjoy your food. In fact, you do not eat to live but, rather, live to eat. It is not surprising, then, to find that your digestive apparatus will be the portion of your body which will give you the most concern.

Do not neglect such ailments as indigestion and, when they come, do not try to cure them by means of drugs. Take moderate exercise such as walking and mild physical jerks. Breathe plenty of fresh air, put yourself on a rational diet and eat fruit.

After fifty years of age, beware of inertia. You will be apt to give up this and that, and grow into an individual who loses his hold on life. Keep up your interest in things, develop your hobbies and remember that nobody can grow old if they mix with younger people than themselves.

Lucky Portents.—People of Taurus derive good luck from the colours blue and any shade incorporating blue, such as violet.

Their mascot should be the emerald and the agate.

Their lucky day of the week is Friday.

The metal which will provide them with most good fortune is copper.

# Were You Born between May 21st and June 21st?

## The Period of Gemini

Gemini rules the period between May 21st and June 21st. Its symbol is a pair of twin children. Mercury is the planet which watches over its destinies.

General Characteristics.—If you were born under the sway of this sign you are more clever than most people. This is due to the fact that you can learn things quickly and without much effort.

You possess a double nature, however. At times, you show that you are endowed with brilliant attainments, you are far-seeing, you are charitable and kind, you are hospitable. But, while all these things are abundantly true, you have another side to your nature which asserts itself on occasion. When the fit overtakes you, you are irritable, quickly roused, easily annoyed and devoid of patience. On such occasions, you are morose, incapable of concentration and cannot execute work up to your usual standard.

The great thing for you to do on these occasions is to practise the art of mastering your own actions. This double nature of yours must and can be conquered by cultivating such qualities as determination. Make up your mind to be strong ; think in terms of strength ; act in terms of strength and shun all that savours of weakness. Learn to be considerate to others so that they need your support, and endeavour to be a little better than the next man or woman, not so that you may crow over them, but in order to give them a helping hand.

While practising determination, do not allow an inferiority complex to creep into your mind. The cure would then be worse than the complaint.

OCCUPATIONS.—You have, above all, a facility for putting thoughts into eloquent words ; thus you would do admirably as a journalist, a lecturer or even a commercial traveller. Never would you be at a loss for something to say. This quality would fit you for a teacher ; but, when your impatient moods overtook you, you would fare very badly.

In almost any occupation requiring quick thinking, you will succeed very well ; but it must not be monotonous work or you will prove an utter failure.

You like change and variety, so that any job which takes you up and down the country, or to some far-flung outpost of Empire, will be appreciated.

If a man, you will fare better as your own master than when working for somebody else. You would hate to have to catch the eight-five train every morning and to sign on at nine. You want to come and go when you like and, to be able to do this, you must be your own master.

HOBBIES AND PASTIMES.—You will take up many hobbies ; you will become very much wrapped-up in them ; then, suddenly you will lose patience and cast them aside. Another will be chosen and it will suffer the same fate in due course. Thus, you will proceed through life.

On the whole, your hobbies will afford you considerable pleasure ; you will learn much from them, seeing that you will sample so many.

LOVE MATTERS.—People of Gemini need love as much as they do food. They are capable of deep affection and make excellent partners. They must guard against marrying someone of a station beneath them, because they lack just the toleration required for making such a union a success.

Women of Gemini are excellent housewives as long as there is abundance of money for the home, but they are not particularly good at pinching and scraping to make both ends meet. When this is necessary, the glamour of their lives fades out and monotony fills its place. Gemini wives need plenty of diversion and their husbands should see to it that they go out a good deal.

DATES.—You will find, during certain periods of the year, that you are able to achieve everything you attempt, whilst at other times things have the habit of taking on a dismal complexion. The good periods are during the passage of Libra, the latter half of Capricorn and the opening days of

Aquarius, as well as a few days before and after your birthday. The dark periods are during Pisces.

LIFE, HEALTH, ETC.—Above all things, you must avoid overwork and overstrain. You are prone to both and your nature is such that they are particularly harmful to you. Be careful to get sufficient sleep and do not plan things while lying in bed. Try to make your mind a total blank then. If possible, look upon the week-end as a time for complete rest and not one in which to do all the odd things that have been held up during the week.

Too much excitement is decidedly bad and a time of hurry and flurry will take more out of you than it will from most people. Therefore, try to live a serene and peaceful life. Do not worry over what cannot be helped.

Gemini people are apt to suffer from such complaints as insomnia, neuralgia, headaches and eye-strain. Many of the children are stammerers.

LUCKY PORTENTS.—The men and women of Gemini derive good luck from yellow and any colour containing yellow, such as green and orange.

Their mascot should be the agate.

Their lucky day of the week is Thursday.

The metal which will bring them most luck is silver.

# Were You Born between June 22nd and July 22nd?

## The Period of Cancer

Cancer rules the period between June 22nd and July 22nd. Its sign is usually delineated as a creature resembling a queer-looking lobster ; but, as the name implies, it should be a crab. The Moon is the planet which guides its destinies.

GENERAL CHARACTERISTICS.—If you were born under the sway of this sign, you are a sensitive and emotional person The hard knocks of this world have more effect on you than they have on most other people, and you lose some of the enjoyment of life in consequence. What other people say and think of you is taken by you to heart. Thus, there are a certain number of things which cause you unhappiness which, after all, are not worth troubling about.

Your manner is quiet, as a rule, and this quality gives you

the appearance of being strong and determined in the eyes of your fellow-men and women. It enables you to get your own way when you want it.

You do not say as much as you think and, while you are thinking, you are reasoning. It follows that your judgment is worth having, and people will flock to you for advice.

While others are accepting your advice and acting on it, it is curious to note that you, yourself, are not so eager to abide by your own judgment. Often, you have not the courage of your own convictions and your actions are not as sound as your advice.

You have several excellent qualities. You are highly sympathetic, which makes you a good friend ; you are loyal and patriotic, and are thus a first-class citizen ; you are, or would be, a most lovable parent. In double harness, again, you are, or would be, everything that your partner could desire. Clearly, the good qualities far outweigh the others.

OCCUPATIONS.—You are not fitted for any calling that is decidedly strenuous, nor do you care for too much responsibility. You do not mind work, in fact work agrees with you, but it must not involve a load of responsibility and it must not come in avalanches.

While you are prepared to turn your hand to almost anything, it is very noticeable that you have a decided flair for all that is cultured and clean. You would much prefer to sell books or diamonds, for instance, to coals or meat, even though the latter might reward you with a much larger income. In addition, you may have noticed that an occupation which brings you in contact with bright lights and a certain amount of gaiety suits you far better than one that relegates you to loneliness and quiet. As a matter of fact, your own quiet nature cannot tolerate quiet surroundings and it yearns for brightness and anything cheery.

Women belonging to this period make excellent caterers. They do well in almost any capacity connected with hotels ; they are first-rate as assistants in large stores, except at sale times ; in theatres and cinemas they find much congenial work and, if they have to fill the post of a clerk in an office, they will be more comfortable where there are forty-nine others than where they sit in the office by themselves.

HOBBIES AND PASTIMES.—You have the bump of acquisition strongly developed. It follows that you like to collect things ; it may be old china, postage stamps—anything. Moreover,

you find it difficult to throw things away or to part with them.

" Ah," you say, " I might want that some day," and you put it aside. Thus, you are a born collector.

Such other hobbies as you have are more of the indoor kind than the outdoor. You have the patience to make things, and if you have not the skill you could easily acquire it.

LOVE MATTERS.—You are not a person who ought to go through life in single blessedness and, as a matter of fact, the older you grow, the more you will need a partner to listen to your joys and your sorrows.

You set much store on a home of your own, and marriage brings this into being in a manner. which you consider more perfect than any other. Your home will be your god. If you are a woman, you will say, when there are children about you, that you were never so completely happy until they came.

You will marry for love, naturally ; but as the years roll on, you will think more and more of your partner, until a time will come when you cannot bear to be separated even for a day or two.

DATES.—You will find, during certain periods of the year, that you are able to achieve almost anything that comes before you, whilst, at others, the exact opposite is the case. It is during the passage of Aquarius and Libra that you have the power to conquer and, during Cancer, that your driving force is least active.

LIFE, HEALTH, ETC.—It would be misleading to say that you are robust ; nevertheless, there is no reason why you should not live to an advanced age, with care. There are two things to watch over : they are indigestion and rheumatism.

Regarding your indigestion, be careful not to hurry over your meals, and eat them in peaceful surroundings. In addition, see that you take them at regular hours.

As regards rheumatism, this need not concern you much as long as you guard against damp air, cold winds, wet feet, and so on.

LUCKY PORTENTS.—You will derive good luck from any shade of green, also grey.

Your mascot should be the ruby.

Your lucky day of the week is Sunday.

Your luck will be enhanced by the metal silver.

# Were You Born between July 23rd and August 22nd?

## The Period of Leo

Leo rules the period between July 23rd and August 22nd. As the name implies, it has the symbol of a lion. The Sun is the planet which guides its destinies.

GENERAL CHARACTERISTICS.—If you were born under the sway of Leo, which is influenced mainly by the Sun, you started out in life under exceptionally favourable circumstances; it might be said that you were born with a silver spoon in your mouth.

You are personally attractive, graceful and refined. You are large-hearted and large-minded. You are forceful in character; you are as meek as a lamb when things take a favourable course, and considerate when things go awry. You are a born leader, but you are too modest to parade this quality. Your memory is unusually good and you never forget a kindness; you are generous, even to excess. You have a methodical nature, which is reflected in your work, your dress and your particular place of abode.

Your ambitions are exalted and you set yourself a very high goal to aim at. Often, you fall short of the mark, as is bound to happen, but what you do achieve is above the average.

You think in big things and act in big things, and you cannot be bothered with niggling details.

If you have any inferior qualities, they lie in the direction of being over-independent. You want to run on your own feet and somewhat resent the help of others. This independence leads to stubbornness and there are times when you will not admit that you are in the wrong. If it is a fault to be too generous, then this is another of your weaknesses.

OCCUPATIONS.—We have all felt, when being in the company of certain men and women, that they were born to lead. They possess a peculiar magnetism which singles them out from their less-fortunate brothers and sisters. Most of them were born under the sway of Leo, as you were.

You have an excellent memory, excellent health, and plenty of force in your character. All this makes it clear that you

were born to command. It hardly matters what the particular line of occupation is, you should do well in it. But where you will chafe is in passing up from the junior posts to the executive positions. If promotion is slow, you may become despondent and even spoil your chances by plain speaking. Once you climb up the ladder and reach a good height, your abilities will establish you firmly. From this, it is seen that you will fare better in the higher ranks of service than in the lower. Clearly, it will be wise for you to go cautiously while getting your footing.

Women are no less excellent leaders than men. We can point to several, who claim allegiance to Leo, who are making well over a thousand pounds a year.

In the home, the women of Leo shine as hostesses and their homes are models of comfort and efficiency.

HOBBIES AND PASTIMES.—The men and women of Leo have strenuous hobbies and pastimes. They play cricket, football, tennis and such games with a zest that amazes the average mortal. They will toil at business all day and, in the evening, play a round of golf as though they had been resting all the afternoon in anticipation of it. They take part in athletic sports, and often carry off the prizes. They will plan a twenty-mile walk, rather than have nothing to occupy an off-day. Their vitality is amazing.

LOVE MATTERS.—In love matters, the men and women of Leo are just as vigorous as they are in work and play. Once they fall in love, they want to be in the company of their intended-one every available minute of the time. They are too wise to neglect their work ; but, once the work is accomplished, they will hurry off to the trysting-place to keep the appointment. Not a minute will be lost.

When marriage is an accomplished fact, the Leo partner will want to rule the home, whether it be the man or the woman. The ruling will not be done, necessarily, in an aggressive manner ; it will certainly be efficient.

Where the woman was born under the influence of Leo, she often helps her husband in his business affairs and this she performs with marked efficiency. Leo people should, for preference, take a partner born under the sway of Pisces ; but Aries, Scorpio and Sagittarius are also good.

DATES.—You will have noticed that, at certain periods of the year, your capabilities for success are much more

marked than they are at other times. These favourable periods come when Pisces and Scorpio are in the ascendancy, the unfavourable ones, while Aquarius is passing. Note these dates and let your actions accord with them.

LIFE, HEALTH, ETC.—The influence of the Sun has impressed itself on your constitution and you have an abundance of vitality. You are robust and not likely to suffer much unless you overtax yourself. Just because you can burn the candle at both ends, you must not think that it is a wise thing to do. Be reasonable with yourself, do not take too much out of the bank of health, and you will have cause for congratulating yourself in later life.

Illness, if it does come, usually comes unexpectedly. Really, it has been coming a long while before it manifests itself. A little hard thinking will show that you plainly asked for the trouble. No doubt, it was something you could have avoided.

LUCKY PORTENTS.—People of Leo derive good luck by using any colour which is based on yellow. Gold is included.

Their mascot is the sardonyx.

Their lucky day is Monday.

Gold, the precious metal, will influence them for good.

# Were You Born between August 23rd and September 22nd?

## The Period of Virgo

Virgo rules the period between August 23rd and September 22nd. For its symbol it has the device of a virgin. Mercury is the planet which guides its destinies.

GENERAL CHARACTERISTICS.—If you were born under the sway of this sign, you have several desirable qualities. First and foremost, you revel in work and there is hardly a limit to the amount you can do. Next, you have your eyes wide open and your brain is alert. Taken together, these qualities single you out as being a very powerful influence in your own sphere of activities.

There is still more to be said. You are wonderfully practical in all you do, and you have a very keen brain for

remembering details. In fact, details mean so much to you that you are apt to irritate some of your co-workers with them. You never forget a face, though you are less accurate in remembering names. The same quality enables you to remember places, and it would not be surprising if you were conversant with every nook and cranny in your own district. Out of this, arises the fact that topography interests you and you could sit over a map for hours and enjoy looking at it.

You are neat in dress and all your possessions are tidily kept and arranged.

You are a person who wants to know the " why and where-fore " of everything. Until you are satisfied on these points, you refrain from acting. Consequently, you miss a good deal, and some people look upon you as a procrastinator.

In a measure you are too sensitive and, often, you hold back when you should go ahead. This unfits you for certain forms of leadership.

You do not want your own way in most things ; in fact you are very amenable, taken all round ; but you do demand that those who come in contact with you should be methodical and orderly. If they are not, you are too ready to show your feelings.

OCCUPATIONS.—There are many forms of work that you could take up with entire success. All those occupations that depend, primarily, on passing examinations are within your range, since you are quick to learn and the " grind " necessary for their success is not a matter that irritates you.

Your capacity for detail is valuable in a thousand widely different jobs. You would make an excellent journalist, not a bad detective ; as a teacher you would be probably very good ; whilst your facility for remembering faces would be a valuable asset as a shopkeeper. What panders more to a customer's vanity than to be able to tell him everything that he discussed on his last visit ? You have a wonderful gift for doing this.

As has been said, you are not exceptionally good in posts where leadership is required ; but you would do well in almost any capacity where decisions have to be made.

You are not fitted for the work of a commercial traveller and, generally speaking, the sea does not attract you.

HOBBIES AND PASTIMES.—You are rich in mental interests and the more cultured arts mean a good deal to you. You

find more pleasure in planning a holiday than in actually going over the itinerary. You love books and reading, and enjoy rambling over a museum rather than across the moors.

LOVE MATTERS.—You take love very seriously ; in fact, you approach it in such a manner that the object of your affections is likely to be frightened away. Once the course of true love runs smoothly, you show that your affections are deep and real. You will make a very sympathetic partner and the person whom you marry will have your undivided love. You will want him or her, however, to listen attentively to your troubles ; but you will not have the patience to give a sympathetic ear to theirs.

DATES.—During certain periods of the year, you will find that there is nothing that you cannot achieve with success ; also, that at other times everything seems to fall flat. This is due to the Zodiacal influence on your particular sign. It is during the passage of Taurus and the first half of Gemini that you are successful, and during Aquarius that the Fates are not kindly disposed.

LIFE, HEALTH, ETC.—While you are not actually robust, there are few reasons, however, why you should be concerned about your health. Your chief ailments will be more imaginary than real. Nevertheless, they will cause you a certain amount of unnecessary anxiety.

People who are Virgo-born are of the introspective kind. They look into themselves too much and wonder why this or that has happened, when, in reality, it is nothing worth thinking twice about. They are apt to read medical books, and their imaginations manufacture the symptoms of dread diseases. They provide the dividends for patent medicine firms.

Avoid drugs, except those prescribed by a doctor ; lead a natural, normal life ; have plenty of sleep ; take sufficient outdoor exercise and eat sensibly.

LUCKY PORTENTS.—Virgo-born people derive good luck by associating themselves with various shades of brown and grey.

Their mascot will be the sapphire.

Their lucky day of the week is Tuesday.

Their metal is silver.

# Were You Born between September 23rd and October 23rd?

## The Period of Libra

Libra rules the period between September 23rd and October 23rd. It has, as its symbol, a pair of scales or a balance. Venus is the planet which guides its destinies.

GENERAL CHARACTERISTICS.—If you were born under the sway of this sign, you are a lover of all that is beautiful, whether it is a work of art, a pleasant landscape or a person of good appearance. Not only do you value beauty as measured by the eye, but you are attracted also by beauty in other forms. Good music appeals to you ; a good character, possessed by an individual, appeals to you ; a tastefully arranged meal appeals to you, and so on. You are, in fact, a connoisseur of everything that is above the ordinary.

You have a gift for making other people happy. You know how to comfort those who are troubled and you know how to make them pleased with themselves. This is a rare gift and there are not enough people like you in the world.

You are not as practical as some people and, in keeping appointments, you are none too punctual. You are somewhat over-sensitive and there are times when you are put-out needlessly. But your displeasure does not show itself in the form of a squabble. Disharmony is a thing you avoid at all costs. Maybe, you nurse a grievance, but this is something that others are never allowed to sense. You keep it strictly to yourself.

OCCUPATIONS.—You are not particularly well suited to a business or commercial life, since these demand a practical nature which you do not possess. Moreover, many of them entail monotony and routine which would grate very harshly on your artistic temperament. Let it be said that, while you would fail in these directions, there are plenty of occupations in which you ought to do remarkably well.

There are many branches in the world of music where you would find congenial work. Literature and the drama may be cited as other suitable outlets for your talents. Women are particularly suited for the finer requirements of dress-making and needlework in general.

Generally speaking, you have an aptitude for several of the highest professions. The law and medicine may be instanced ; but, while mentioning the latter, it must be admitted that some of the pathetic sights which the doctor sees might shake your finely-balanced temperament. Roughing it is not in your line.

HOBBIES AND PASTIMES.—Your leisure moments must be spent in a manner fitting to your temperament. Seeing that you value refinement and comforts, you do not care for rough or strenuous games. You like the company of others and you seek the " bright-spots " of life. Card-playing, probably, tempts you, but it has no attractions unless money stakes are involved. And, here, it may be well to warn you against gambling. If allowed, it might take a strong hold on you.

LOVE MATTERS.—There is no doubt that Libra-born people should marry, if they are to enjoy the life that fits their natures best. Solitude and loneliness are death to them, and, given suitable companionship, they are very charming people. They want to marry young. They should choose someone who is cheerful and entertaining as a partner. The choice should be made in favour of a person born during their own Zodiacal period.

Libra people require a home that is tastefully arranged and which reveals nothing of a sordid nature. They cannot hear makeshifts.

Their chief trouble arises out of their fundamental qualities. The complex situation may be stated briefly, thus : They wish to marry early and they engage in work that is not highly remunerative in the commencing years. Thus, they are not well off in the initial stages. Yet they are disappointed at having to put up with makeshifts. Clearly, they require a certain amount of strength of will to pull them through the first few years of married life.

DATES.—You will find, during certain periods of the year, that you are able to achieve everything you desire and, at other times, things habitually take on an adverse complexion. This is only to be expected once the Zodiacal influences have been appreciated. Your best periods are during the passage of Gemini and Aquarius, and your worst during Cancer.

LIFE, HEALTH, ETC.—Those who are Libra-born are well-favoured as far as their constitutions are concerned ; but they are liable to suffer from nervous disorders and indigestion. The first is the direct outcome of their highly sensitive natures.

They become exhausted more quickly than the average person and the life they enjoy does not help in the matter.

Digestive troubles result from self-indulgence. Too much is eaten; what is eaten is too rich and, very often, it is eaten too late in the day. There is a tendency to corpulence in later life.

LUCKY PORTENTS.—If you are born under the sign of Libra, you will gain a distinct advantage in surrounding yourself with browns and greens, also blues.

Your lucky mascot should be the opal.

Your lucky day of the week is Friday.

There is no special metal to which you may look for good fortune.


# Were You Born between October 24th and November 22nd?

## The Period of Scorpio

Scorpio rules the period between October 24th and November 22nd. A scorpion serves for its sign. Mars is the planet which rules its destinies.

GENERAL CHARACTERISTICS.—If you were born under the sway of this sign, you are something of an enigma. The only person who really knows you is yourself. You have the power of acting a part in life that is totally different from your true self.

One thing is definite. You possess considerable magnetic power and you can use it for good or for ill. How you do use it depends entirely on your own desires. Fortunately, the people who were born under the influence of Scorpio, being strong, are usually able to control their actions for good and the result is that their magnetic power sheds a beneficial influence on others. Those who tread the path of evil are, naturally, very dangerous people.

Loyal and upright Scorpio-born individuals are large in mind and large in heart. They need success for themselves and are ever ready to help others to gain it as well. They value happiness and know how to obtain it ; but they would scorn the thought of getting it at someone else's expense. In fact, they devote their energies towards securing it for their fellow-creatures.

They are sympathetic, hard-working, generous and friendly ; but they are quick to be roused. When their tempers get the best of them, they lose all control and make assertions for which they are sorry later on. Obviously, even the best of them need more self-control.

OCCUPATIONS.—Your inherent " push and go " are very useful acquirements. Whilst others are debating, you are acting, and it is the early bird that gets the worm. You should cast away all thought of taking up a profession or occupation that requires polish and genteelness. You are far too practical to bother about surface qualities ; they irritate you. You are a person of action and prefer rough and ready efficiency to anything else.

You could play the part of an explorer admirably, both in real life and on the films. You would be far better as a veterinary surgeon than as a Harley Street consultant. At any job where skill in making things was needed, you would succeed. Engineering may be cited as such a job. There are many occupations at sea which would suit you extraordinarily well. As an aviator, you would display the requisite pluck and daring. There are endless fields for your energies in work connected with land. Not only would you make an excellent farmer, but you would do equally well as a surveyor, a mining engineer and a prospector.

Women are suited to most of the occupations above mentioned, as well as to cookery and laundry work.

HOBBIES AND PASTIMES.—Vigorous pastimes attract you most and they do you the most good. A really fast game at football, tennis, etc., is a capital outlet for your energies and you will be all the better for it. You will like walking when middle-age is reached, but you will think more of a fourteen than a four mile walk. On holidays, you will not want to sit on the beach and wait for the next meal, with only a newspaper to amuse you. The most distant hills on the landscape will beckon to you, and you will want to know what they look like close to.

LOVE MATTERS.—There is no such thing as a platonic friendship where Scorpio-people are concerned. When they love, they love with an ardour that is unquenchable. They seldom change their affections, once they have been definitely expressed. Anyone in the rôle of a rival is dealt with ruthlessly and, maybe, with force.

He or she who marries a Scorpio must give no cause for

jealousy, since this is a point on which the Scorpio-born are extremely sensitive. In all other respects, they are admirable partners and they usually idolise the one they marry.

The women make excellent wives, but they often wish to rule the roost and woe-betide the husband who makes a practice of visiting his club too frequently.

The Scorpio-born should marry another of the same Zodiacal period.

DATES.—You will find during certain periods of the year that you are able to achieve everything to which you put your hand while, at other times, things are apt to turn out badly. The good periods are during the passage of Pisces and Cancer ; the unfavourable ones, during Leo. Naturally, these periods should be regulated to accord with your important actions.

LIFE, HEALTH, ETC.—You have a strong constitution, but are apt to overtax it with work and play. Everything you do, you do strenuously, so that the life you lead takes too much out of you. Be calmer in your actions ; be more deliberate ; take a few minutes longer over walking to the station and in eating your meals. Never cut down the hours of sleep, and avoid working overtime as much as possible. Take as long holidays as you can and plan them to be restful.

It is your heart that will be the first organ to trouble you should illness come. If it is overtaxed it will rebel against your method of life, but it will do so mildly on the first occasion. Take warning of the very first signs of trouble, for the next occasion will be more serious.

LUCKY PORTENTS.—Were you born during the passage of Scorpio, then associate yourself with such colours as dark red and crimson.

Your mascot should be the topaz or the malachite.

Your lucky day of the week is Tuesday.

There is no special metal which will assist your fortunes.

# Were You Born between
# November 23rd and December 21st ?

## The Period of Sagittarius

Sagittarius rules the period between November 23rd and December 21st. Its symbol is a centaur—a creature, half

man and half horse—who is shooting an arrow into the air. Jupiter is the planet which guides its destinies.

GENERAL CHARACTERISTICS.—If you were born under the sway of this sign, you have a certain amount of philosophy in your character ; but it lies dormant a good deal of the time. You are large-hearted and sincere, though a trifle blunt. You are somewhat proud and people who pander to your vanity become your best friends. You have high ideals which cannot be always realised. When they fail, you allow yourself to be considerably dejected. You are far-seeing and make an excellent leader. There is a streak of restlessness in your " make-up," which causes you to cast aside an ideal before it has had sufficient time to mature. Consequently, you do not attain the success in life, nor the happiness and comfort, that your qualities merit.

You know how to express your opinions in public and you have a neat gift for being humorous. It follows that you are credited by your friends as being jolly good company. Certainly you are entertaining. Your friends, by the way, have considerable influence on you and it is highly necessary that you should choose them wisely and deliberately.

Your greatest failing is that you are too versatile and that your energies are directed into too many channels. Concentrate on fewer branches of work and pleasure, and you will greatly benefit by the change.

OCCUPATIONS.—Whatever you turn to, you will engage in with all your might—for a time. Then, if monotony or routine plays a large part in the chosen occupation, you will become restless and look for a complete change. Accordingly, you must see to it that, at the outset, you choose a form of work possessing plenty of variety. You should think of nothing that keeps you seated in an office, since you need movement.

There is much in a commercial traveller's work that will appeal to you ; but there are thousands of kindred jobs, which will take you from place to place and where you will be constantly seeing fresh faces, that will be suited to your requirements, also.

The Sagittarian should aim at entering on work in which he or she can be his or her own master eventually. These people have executive ability which fits them for ruling in their own right after they reach the age of 35. Moreover, at about this time, they become unfitted for serving under others.

Women have not quite as much restlessness in their natures as men, though it is there just the same. Accordingly, they can put up with monotony, as long as it is not too pronounced. For them, any occupation in which they can create things is suitable. Thus, dressmaking, millinery, and any art and craft work may be recommended.

HOBBIES AND PASTIMES.—Outdoor pursuits engage much of your leisure time and you find them exceedingly beneficial. The fear is that you may overdo them and harm your constitution.

You love movement in the open ; thus, if horse-riding does not attract you, it is certain that you enjoy the pleasures of fast motoring or, perhaps, a long journey in a train, as well as a trip on a pleasure cruise.

You take a keen interest in educating yourself, using books or educational visits for the purpose. More than likely you gain far more satisfaction than knowledge from the effort.

LOVE MATTERS.—You never forget friends ; consequently, you have a large circle of acquaintances, many of them speaking a foreign tongue. From among this large circle you will choose a partner, if you have not already done so. Usually, the choice will surprise those who know you best.

You will marry and be comfortable ; but marriage will not be everything to you, as it is to most people. Other diversions will vie with it and take your interests away from the home. Should your partner endeavour to curb this inclination, it may lead to a possible rupture.

DATES.—At certain times of the year, you are able to accomplish everything that you attempt, while, at others, your successes are few and far between. These periods are determined by Zodiacal influence and are beyond your control. The good periods come during the first half of the passage of Pisces and Aries and during the whole of Cancer. The less fortunate occasions are during the latter half of Pisces and Aries.

LIFE, HEALTH, ETC.—To be born under Sagittarius is to have a good constitution. You possess a considerable amount of vitality and it will be preserved well into old age, if you take plenty of outdoor exercise ; but this can be easily overdone. Should you exceed a reasonable amount, trouble will manifest itself in the breathing apparatus and will lead to bronchial diseases.

You are liable to attacks of sciatica and rheumatism after

56 years of age. It will be difficult to assign a reason for these attacks, but manifestly they are due to exposing yourself too frequently to the night air.

Women should not indulge in any sport that involves speed after they have reached 45 years of age. They are unfitted to cope with the strain.

LUCKY PORTENTS.—You will derive good luck by surrounding yourself with the colour purple.

Your mascot should be the turquoise.

Your lucky day of the week is Wednesday.

You will gain favours by associating your fortunes with the metal tin.

# THE ORACLE OF DESTINY

This table is to be tried on any day of the week, Wednesdays excepted, which is held by the Greek sages and the professors of the noble science of Astrology as unlucky for such pursuits, casting nativities, or interpreting dreams. How far they may

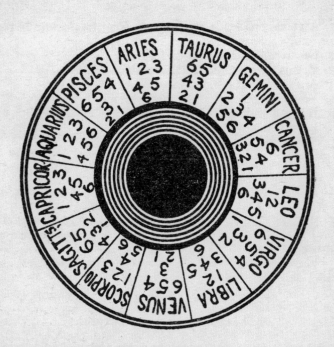

The Oracle of Destiny

be right, the translator does not pretend to judge : it is certain they maintain that opinion. Also, that no person should search into the knowledge of future events on their natal day.

Prick in the table, with your eyelids closed, for the planet that is to fall to your share, and, having found it out, note the number that decides your destiny. What it means is given below.

173

## Aquarius

1. A happy lot, especially in matrimony.
2. Several lovers, and select the worst.
3. An unexpected event that will enrich you.
4. You will benefit more by the dead than by the living.
5. You will be enriched through the means of a foreigner whom you have not yet seen.
6. Every stroke of ill luck will be quickly followed by a slice of good fortune.

## Pisces

1. A good conscience will be your chief treasure in old age, after many changes.
2. Great benefit from good children.
3. Voyages to sea, and settlement abroad.
4. A great loss through a false friend or lover.
5. You will better yourself in marriage.
6. If you a widowhood should gain,
   Long you will not it retain,
   You're born to a third marriage chain.

## Aries

1. If you do not get rich by your twenty-ninth year, you never will, for that is your utmost elevation.
2. A speedy prosperity when you think Fate has deserted you, by most unlooked-for but honest means—so do not despair.
3. Face danger boldly. You are born to surmount difficulties, and have a happy meridian and end.
4. You will gain experience rather too dear, but prosper after your lesson.
5. Jealousy will be the spoiler of your peace.
6. You will not wed your first love, but the loss is all for the best.

## Taurus

1. You will have riches, but an ill-tempered mate.
2. Within a month you will find something of consequence.
3. Several children, but not to your bliss.
4. A debt contracted by imprudence that will annoy you.
5. Important news on the road from afar.
6. A strange home within a year.

## GEMINI

1. A new lover, but a constant and valuable one.
2. Perfidy is about to wound you.
3. There's a person has made a promise which you depend on, and they intend to keep it, but will not be able, so prepare your mind.
4. Many flowers in your path.
5. Deceit from an unexpected quarter.
6. A foreign letter of interest.

## CANCER

1. Great promotion at hand.
2. An enviable fate is to come.
3. A speedy change in present affairs.
4. A failure in trade to your detriment.
5. A sincere friend of the other sex.
6. A party of pleasure, from which great events will arise.

## LEO

1. A moonlight walk will be long remembered.
2. Many changes at hand.
3. A quarrel with your lover.
4. You have a secret rival.
5. You have a false confidant.
6. The next favour you ask will be granted.

## VIRGO

1. Gives you prosperity and the chance of a number in Capricorn.
2. Gives you comforting children and mark 3 in Capricorn.
3. Two husbands.
4. A speedy offer you had best reject.
5. The loss of what you can never regain.
6. Speedy reconciliation when you desire it.

## LIBRA

1. You will gain many useful friends.
2. Refers you to Capricorn to try a number.
3. You will suffer by scandal.
4. You will go abroad within three years.
5. You will suffer by carelessness.
6. You will lose by a wager.

## Venus

1. Early marriage for the single. Happiness to all.
2. Too many lovers, and some tears.
3. Crossings in love and amorous perplexities.
4. An intrigue stopped in good time.
5. A false lover and a perfidious friend.
6. Advancement through marriage.

## Scorpio

1. A bustling life, but little advancement.
2. A better end than beginning.
3. Success by trade or servitude.
4. A sudden or happy elevation.
5. A new offer and a new establishment.
6. Sagittarius No. 3 gives the answer.

## Sagittarius

1. Your planets give a happy issue to your own endeavours —depend not on others for support.
2. An easy life, with few cares to depress you.
3. Your planets give strife and discord.
4. Your partner will be too fond of pleasures.
5. You will soon form a lasting friendship.
6. You will soon gain what you most desire.

## Capricorn

1. The best of blessings—health and happiness.
2. An excellent offer will soon be made to your advantage.
3. Unexpected prosperity from persons at present unknown.
4. Fate has good things in store for you.
5. You will sow with toil, and reap a golden harvest.
6. You will soon have cause to rejoice.

# DREAMS AND WHAT THEY MEAN

*In sleep, the soul is free from the hamperings of the body and its limitations. The soul then knows what happened to it in its previous lives. It lives these over again in recollection. It has glimpses here and there of its past experiences. Some of these are dimly remembered and brought over to the waking consciousness. In other cases, the soul, knowing its own immortality, is able to glean and bring back some ideas of its immediate future. It knows what is to happen, and tries to warn and guide its gross vehicle aright—to direct it amid the stream of impressions it is receiving minute by minute which distract it and lead it astray.*

JAMES WARD.

**Abbey.**—This denotes future comfort, peace of mind, freedom from anxiety.

**Abroad.**—To dream of being abroad, denotes a removal.

**Abscess.**—A sure sign of coming success and good fortune.

**Absent Friends.**—To dream that they are alive, but ill, indicates bad news; that they are well denotes they are prosperous; that they are dead, foretells good news relating to a wedding.

**Abuse.**—To dream that you are abused, denotes that a dispute will arise between you and someone with whom you do business, or with your lover.

**Accident.**—Injury of any part of your body, denotes coming personal affliction from which you will recover. If an accident at sea, you will be crossed in love.

**Accuse.**—To dream that you are accused of a crime of which you are found guilty, is a sign of great trouble ; if not guilty, you will acquire riches.

**Ache.**—Aches and pains denote a temporary illness.

**Acorns.**—Health, strength, and worldly abundance.

**Actress.**—For a man to dream of an actress, it shows that he is about to become prosperous.

**Admire.**—To dream that you admire a person is an omen that your lover is sincere. To dream that you are admired betokens numerous friends.

**Adultery.**—Dreaming of a successful resistance, intimates that you will prosper ; of being guilty, your prospects in love will be blasted.

**Advancement.**—If you dream that you are advanced in your situation, it is a sign of success in all you undertake.

**Adversity.**—To dream of being in adverse circumstances, generally indicates the reverse, prosperity.

**Advice.**—Receiving advice, denotes difficulties; but wise and faithful friends to help you. Giving advice, is a sign that you will be highly esteemed by others.

**Aeroplane.**—To dream of any air vessel is a warning against taking risks.

**Affluence.**—Frequently found to denote the contrary.

**Afraid.**—You will succeed. Your lover will prove true.

**Age.**—A dream about your age betokens sickness, and premature death.

**Ague.**—To dream that you have the ague denotes constant changes in your business and circumstances.

**Air.**—Dreaming of being in the air, floating about in it, means that you will progress through monetary gains. To be surrounded by foggy air indicates uncertainty —concerning your greatest desires.

**Alligator.**—This denotes a sly, crafty enemy; you should exercise caution.

**Alms.**—If begged of you, and you fail to respond, you will experience misery. To give freely, points to much future happiness.

**Amputation.**—A warning of the death of someone near and dear.

**Anchor.**—All in water, implies disappointment. Part in water, foretells a voyage.

**Angels.**—You will have prosperity, peace, and happiness.

**Anger.**—If angry with some person, it is sign that that person is your best friend. To dream that your lover is angry with you, portends true love and happiness.

**Annoy.**—To dream that you are annoyed, denotes that you have enemies about you.

**Ants.**—Foretells removal to a large mercantile city where, if you are industrious, you will accumulate riches. To those in love it foretells a speedy marriage and a large family. To those in business, increased trade and ultimate independence.

**Arms.**—To dream that the arms are cut off or missing, denotes sickness.

**Army.**—To see an army or any large company of soldiers who are victorious suggests good-fortune for you; if they are defeated, you will experience bad luck.

**Arrow.**—If it penetrates your body, some person or persons are designing your ruin.

**Ascend.**—To dream that you ascend a hill, and reach the top, denotes that you will conquer your difficulties.

**Ashes.**—Foretells some great misfortune.

**Ass.**—Denotes that troubles will have a happy termination.

**Asylum.**—To dream that you are an inmate of an asylum, denotes coming personal affliction.

**Baby.**—To dream that you are nursing a baby denotes sorrow and misfortune, and disappointment in love. To dream that you see a baby that is sick, foretells the death of one of the family.

**Bacon.**—Eating bacon portends sorrow. Buying it foretells the death of a friend, or a quarrel with your lover.

**Badger.**—Long life and great prosperity; much travel in your own and foreign countries.

**Bagpipes.**—Seen and heard in a dream, denote extreme poverty, and unhappy marriage.

**Bald.**—To dream of baldness portends approaching sickness. For a young woman to dream

that her lover is bald, foretells that he will not live to marry her. To dream that she is bald herself, implies she will be very poor, and die an old maid.

**Ball.**—To play with a ball is a sign that you will receive some money, unexpectedly.

**Bankrupt.**—To dream of insolvency, is a dream of warning, lest you should undertake something injurious to yourself.

**Basin.**—Eating or drinking out of a basin, denotes that you will soon be in love; but you may not marry the first object of your affections.

**Bat.**—To dream of seeing a bat flying in the air signifies that you have an enemy. If it appears flying by daylight you need not fear, but if by night, you are in danger.

**Bathing.**—If you dream that you are bathing, and that the water is clear and transparent, prosperity and success in business, and in love will be yours; but if the water be dirty and muddy, you will have nothing but poverty, misfortune, sorrow, and very poor health.

**Bazaar.**—To dream that you are walking through an Eastern bazaar is a sign that you will move from your present abode, in the near future.

**Beach.**—To be sitting on a beach means that you are about to experience loneliness.

**Beans.**—To dream of beans is unfortunate. If you dream of eating them it foretells sickness. If you dream of seeing them growing, it foretells contention with those you love best.

**Bear.**—If you dream of seeing a bear, expect great vexations. To dream that you are fighting with a bear, and kill it, is a favourable sign of your overcoming a formidable foe.

**Bed.**—To dream of being in bed signifies a very early marriage; of making a bed indicates a change of residence.

**Bees.**—To dream of bees is good; it denotes that your industry and enterprise in trade will be very successful.

**Bells.**—To dream of hearing bells ring is a sign of coming good news.

**Blood.**—To dream of blood is very bad, if you see it upon yourself; if on others, it denotes a sudden death to some of the family, loss of property, or severe disappointment.

**Boat.**—If in a boat and the water is smooth, it is a lucky omen denoting prosperous business, and happiness in the marriage state. If the water is rough and muddy, you will have to labour all your life. If you fall into the water, you will meet with great peril in the future.

**Bones.**—Dreaming of bones denotes property; if they are partly covered with flesh, you will grow rich by degrees. To dream of human bones foretells that you will become rich through the death of some relative or friend.

**Books.**—A good sign; your future will be very happy.

**Boots.**—If wearing a new pair of boots and they hurt, it is a sign that you will meet with difficulties caused by your own imprudence.

**Bottle.**—A bottle full of wine indicates your future prosperity; if the bottle be empty, you have an enemy in possession of a secret, which if revealed will do you a deal of harm.

**Box.**—If opening a box, and looking for something in it, and cannot find it, you are going to be troubled about

money matters; or you will suffer some pecuniary loss.

**Bracelet.**—If wearing a bracelet, you will shortly be married to a wealthy person. If you find a bracelet, it is sign of a coming fortune.

**Brambles.**—To dream of briars and brambles denotes many difficulties, poverty and privation all your life. If not hurt by them, you will have trouble of short duration.

**Bread.**—To dream of seeing a quantity of bread is a sign of competency in temporal things. If you dream of eating good bread, you will enjoy good health, and live long; but if the bread is burned or sad, it is a bad sign, and generally portends a funeral. To dream of baking bread is also bad, generally denoting sorrow.

**Breath.**—To dream you are out of breath, or have difficult breathing, is a sign that your health is about to give way.

**Brewing.**—If you dream that you are brewing, you may expect the visit of some distant friend.

**Bride, Bridesmaid, or Bridegroom.**—This is a dream of contrary. To dream that you take any of these characters is a sure forerunner of grief and disappointment.

**Bridge.**—To walk over a broken bridge betokens fear: to dream you fall upon a bridge is a sign of obstruction in business.

**Brothers.**—To dream that you are conversing with your brothers betokens vexations.

**Bugle.**—Hearing a bugle call denotes unexpected news from abroad of a very pleasing nature; and to married persons it denotes the birth of a child.

**Bull.**—To dream that you are pursued by a mad bull, denotes that you will be in danger of losing your friends. If in love, your intended will be in some great danger.

**Burns.**—A dream of contrary, implying health, happiness and friendship.

**Butter.**—To dream of butter, in any way, or form, is a good dream and indicates joy and feasting. To the lover it is a sign of early marriage.

**Butterflies.**—To see these in a dream is a sure sign of coming wealth and luxury.

**C a b b a g e.**—To dream of cabbages in any form, is a sign of healthy and long life for you.

**Cakes.**—If oat-cakes, it denotes health and strength; if sweet cakes, coming joy; if making spicy cakes and bread, an approaching marriage at which you will meet with your lover. To dream of cakes twice denotes your own marriage in which you will be extremely happy.

**Calm.**—To dream of a calm succeeding a storm indicates the reconciliation of separated friends; the end of trouble; the commencement of peace.

**Camels.**—Heavy burdens which you will bear with heroism; but you will eventually become very happy.

**Canary.**—To hear a canary sing denotes marriage and a comfortable habitation.

**Cats.**—An unfavourable dream denoting treachery and deceit.

**Chains.**—If confined in chains, it betokens severe trials for a time, from which you will be extricated. To dream that a person puts a gold chain upon your neck, indicates great favour; and to the lover, marriage.

**Cheese.**—Deception and infidelity in a lover. If the cheese be mity, it denotes numerous

meddling persons who will annoy you. Eating cheese betokens regret for having acted imprudently.

**Children.**—Success in trade, and increase of wealth. To dream that you see your child die, is a dream of contrary; the child will live.

**Church.**—To dream that you go to church in mourning, denotes a wedding; if you go in white, it denotes a funeral.

**Clock.**—To dream you hear a clock strike, denotes a speedy marriage.

**Clouds.**—Dark clouds indicate sorrows which, if the clouds break, will pass away.

**Clothes.**—If a sailor dreams that he has lost his clothes by shipwreck, it is a sign of marriage; otherwise, a dream of contrary.

**Clover.**—If you are in a field of clover, it is an omen that you will do well, enjoy health, and be very happy.

**Coal.**—To dream of coal is a sign that you are going to overcome troubles by being thrifty; but there will be afflictions and losses before the difficulties pass away.

**Coffee.**—Denotes prosperity, and great happiness. To a single person it promises a faithful, affectionate, and confiding lover.

**Coffin.**—A sign of the death of some dear one.

**Colliery.**—To dream that you are near a coalpit, denotes that you will be exposed to danger, and to dream that you are in a coalpit, is a sign that you cannot escape.

**Concert.**—Disagreement among relations.

**Cooking.**—Dreaming of cooking denotes a convivial party, and also the wedding of some friend.

**Corks.**—Corking bottles indicates a favourable change in your circumstances. If you draw corks, it is a sign of the visit of some particular friend.

**Cow.**—To dream that you are pursued by a cow, denotes an enemy; if you escape it you will defeat your enemy. To dream of milking a cow is a sign of abundance.

**Crabs.**—To dream of a crab denotes reverses; and to a sailor, danger of shipwreck and drowning.

**Crown.**—To dream of a monarch's crown, denotes elevation in your state. To wear a royal crown, denotes degradation. To dream that you give a crown, shows that you will rise to independence.

**Crows.**—The sign of a funeral.

**Cuckoo.**—Temporary disappointments in love. If the cuckoo stutters, you will not succeed in business or love. To the married it is the omen of widowhood.

**Cucumbers.**—For the afflicted to dream of cucumbers denotes speedy restoration to health. To a single person, it denotes a happy engagement and marriage.

**Dance.**—You will be the recipient of great favour and honour; your plans will succeed; you will marry well.

**Dark.**—If in darkness and cannot find your way, it denotes a change for the worse in your affairs. If you emerge from the darkness, and behold the sun, it denotes ultimate happiness.

**Dead.**—To dream of those who are dead, denotes mental anguish. If you dream that they are happy, it is a sign favourable to you.

**Death.**—This is a dream of contrary; it augurs happy, long life.

**Dinner.**—If you are getting your dinner, it foretells straits and difficulties.

**Disaster.**—You will hear of the exaltation of some friend in whom you are interested, and it will lead to a marriage. Disaster at sea is a favourable dream for a business man.

**Distance.**—To dream that you are at a distance from your friends, foretells family quarrels, and alienation. To dream of any friend at a distance, indicates that you will hear agreeably of them.

**Divorce.**—If a married person dreams of sueing for a divorce, it is a sign of the fidelity of his or her partner.

**Docks.**—To dream that you are standing by docks, denotes favourable news from abroad.

**Doctor.**—To dream of your doctor is a good omen. It tells of good fortune and health, and may easily include a rise in your status.

**Dogs.**—If a dog fondles with you, you will meet with faithful friends. If he bites you, your best friend will become your greatest enemy. If it only barks at you, you will quarrel with your friend or lover.

**Dress.**—Buying a dress, denotes advancement, and that you will obtain your wishes.

**Drink.**—Drinking at a fountain is a sign of much happiness. If the water is muddy, it denotes approaching trouble. If you are thirsty, and cannot find water, it portends that trials will have to be borne without assistance. You will need self-reliance.

**Driving.**—If you dream of driving any vehicle, expect losses in trade. To dream that someone is driving you in a car, foretells a marriage.

**Drown.**—To dream that you are drowning denotes over-whelming difficulties, losses in trade, and through death. If you are rescued, some friend will help you out of your difficulties.

**Drum.**—To hear a drum, is a sign of national and family turmoils, or that the country will be afflicted with war.

**Ducks.**—If you see the ducks flying, it is an omen of the increase of riches; if you see them swimming on glassy water, it is a sign of peace, and plenty. If you see them dive and bring up worms, it denotes a life of drudgery. To see a duck and drake augurs that your wished-for marriage will soon take place.

**Duel.**—If you have visions of a duel, whether you are engaged in it or not, it is a sign that you will win despite any rival you may have in love affairs.

**Dust.**—To be almost blinded with dust, indicates the failure of your business, and the dispersion of your family. But if you get clear of it, you will recover your former state.

**Dwarf.**—If you see a dwarf, it is a sign that you will be elevated in rank. If you dream that you are a dwarf, it denotes health, muscular strength, and independence.

**Earthquake.**—This foretells much trouble to the dreamer; losses in trade; bereavement; family quarrels.

**Eggs.**—To dream of seeing a great number of eggs, indicates success in trade and in love. It also denotes a happy marriage, good children, and great prosperity. If the eggs prove rotten, it denotes a treacherous friend or lover. To dream of eating eggs portends great enjoyment.

**Elephant.**—Denotes health and strength; and that you will associate with Society.

**Elopement.**—To dream that you are eloping with your lover, indicates you will have a bad partner. If you dream that your lover has eloped with someone else, a rival is likely to supplant you. To dream of a relative or friend eloping denotes their marriage, or news of a sudden death.

**Evergreens.**—Lasting happiness! Lasting love! Lasting honour! Domestic bliss! Fresh engagements will be crowned with success.

**Exile.**—To dream that you are banished, implies that you will have to travel much.

**Farthing.**—To dream that you are not worth a farthing, or that someone gives you a farthing, portends a coming down in the world.

**Fat.**—To dream of getting fat, forebodes some ill to befall you.

**Fawn.**—A sign of inconstancy.

**Feasting.**—Disappointments, enemies, great lowness of spirit, sickness.

**Fighting.**—Disagreements and quarrels in families; misunderstandings among lovers.

**Fire.**—Health and great happiness, kind relations, and warm friends. But if burned with the fire, it portends calamity.

**Fishing.**—To dream that you are fishing and obtain no fish, is an omen of bad success in business, or in love. If you angle them, it augurs the acquisition of riches. If you see the fishes at the bottom of the water, it being very clear, it is a sign of wealth.

**Fortune.**—If you dream that one has left you a fortune, it is a sign that he will not. If that your friend has a fortune, it is a sign of his coming poverty.

**Fountain.**—A muddy fountain indicates trouble. A crystal.

overflowing fountain, denotes abundance, freedom from want.

**Fowls.**—To dream of fowls denotes moderate comfort in temporal things; but in love, you will meet with slander and rivalry.

**Fox.**—If you dream of a fox, you have a sly, lurking enemy.

**Frogs.**—These creatures show that deceit is damaging your reputation.

**Fruit.**—To dream of fruit has a different interpretation according to what the fruit is that you dream of. But to dream of a collection of numerous and varied fruits, both English and foreign, portends unbounded acquisition of wealth—and an agreeable and wealthy matrimonial alliance. The various fruits have different prognostications, thus :

*Apples* betoken long life and success, a boy to a woman with child, faithfulness in your sweetheart, and riches by trade.

*Apricots* denote health and prosperity, a speedy marriage, dutiful children, and success in love.

*Blackberries.*—To dream that you are gathering blackberries to eat, indicates approaching sickness. If you see others gathering them, you have enemies where you least expect them, and who will strive to injure you in your business.

*Cherries* indicate disappointments in love, vexation in the married state.

*Currants* prefigure happiness in life, success in undertakings, constancy in your sweetheart, handsome children to the married, and riches to the farmer and tradesman.

*Elderberries* augur content and riches; to a maiden they bespeak a speedy marriage; to a

married woman, that she will shortly be with child ; to the tradesman, success in business ; to the farmer, good crops.

*Figs* are the forerunners of prosperity and happiness ; to the lover they denote the accomplishment of one's wishes ; to the tradesman, increase of trade ; they are also indicative of a legacy.

*Gooseberries* indicate many children, chiefly sons, and an accomplishment of your present pursuits ; to the sailor they declare dangers in his next voyage ; to the maiden, a roving husband ; and to the man, a rakish wife.

*Grapes* foretell to the maiden that her husband will be a cheerful companion ; they denote much happiness in marriage, and success in trade.

*Lemons* denote contentions in your family and uneasiness on account of children ; the death of some relation, and disappointment in love.

*Medlars* bespeak riches to the dreamer ; to the lover, they foretell a good husband or wife, with beautiful children and much happiness.

*Melons* announce speedy recovery to those who are sick ; settlement of a dispute between you and others ; in love, they announce constancy ; and in marriage, a happy partner, and handsome children.

*Mulberries* foretell a speedy and happy marriage ; they are particularly favourable to sailors and farmers.

*Oranges* forebode loss of goods and reputation, attacks from thieves, wounds, and sickness in the object of your affections.

*Peaches* denote that your love is returned ; riches to the tradesman, good crops to the farmer,

and a prosperous voyage to the sailor.

*Pears.*—Deceit ; (to eat) news of a death ; (to gather) coming happiness.

*Pomegranate.*—A happy augury ; honours will come to you.

**Glass.**—To look clearly through glass, denotes the successful and even tenor of your way. If it is dim and not transparent, your prospects are very uncertain.

**Gloves.**—To lose your gloves denotes loss in business, and a change of abode ; to lose your right glove, if married, you will lose your partner ; if single, another will deprive you of your lover.

**Goats.**—You will have enemies, and many trials through deceit ; but events will operate for your good.

**Gold.**—A sign of poverty and distress.

**Goose.**—Forebodes incompatibility with one's marriage partner.

**Grain.**—To see a quantity of grain implies that you will become wealthy and be greatly respected and honoured.

**Grass.**—To see green grass, denotes great and continued prosperity ; withered and decayed grass is a sign of sickness and distress, probably to one whom you love.

**Grave.**—A dream about an open grave is a sign of some evil overtaking a friend.

**Hams.**—You will be very happy in the domestic circle ; will love and be beloved.

**Handcuffs.**—There is a bad prospect before you. If a lover dreams of being handcuffed to another person, it denotes miserable matrimony.

**Hares.**—To see a hare pursued by dogs portends enemies. To see a few hares, denotes choice and faithful friends. If a hare

runs towards you, it denotes the visit of a dear friend. To a swain or maiden, it is the portent of an early and happy marriage.

**Hay.**—This dream stands for happiness and success.

**Hills.**—To dream of ascending and unable to arrive at the top, is a sign that you will have to labour and toil all your life, have many difficulties and troubles.

**Home.**—To dream of the home of your childhood, indicates health and prosperity. To the lover, it betokens a happy marriage.

**Honey.**—To dream you are eating honey denotes good health, long life, prosperity.

**Horse.**—To dream of a horse is, in general, a sign of success. A white one will be more fortunate than a black one, while brown horses are almost as good as white ones.

**Ice.**—Foretells failure in trade, unsuccessful speculation and enterprise. Your now ardent lover is about to jilt you. To the sailor, it denotes disasters at sea.

**Ill.**—To dream that you are ill, denotes that you are in danger of falling into a great temptation, which, if you do not resist, will injure your character.

**Ink.**—To dream that you are using ink denotes prosperity in business; if you spill it, your correspondence will not be successful, whether in trade or in love.

**Island.**—To dream that you are on a desolate island implies the death of your lover. If a fertile island, your present lover will prove unfaithful; but you will soon meet with a more favourable match.

**Ivy.**—To dream of ivy is a sign that your friend, your lover, your husband, or wife, will adhere to you as ivy clings to the wall. You will have good health and live long.

**Jewels.**—The harbinger of great prosperity, affection, and happy union.

**Journey.**—That you have to go to some distant country, foretells a great change in your circumstances.

**Joy.**—You will receive a sum of money, or become rich through the inheritance of an unexpected legacy from a distant relative.

**Key.**—To lose a key, denotes disappointment and displeasure. To give a key, denotes a marriage; to find or receive one, the birth of a child; to dream of many keys, denotes riches.

**King.**—That you speak to a sovereign, indicates that you will rise to honour and dignity. If the monarch is unfriendly, the dream is unfavourable.

**Kiss.**—Kissing one whom you should not, denotes a false friend or lover. To see another kiss your intended, portends a rival. To see your lover kiss another, denotes a false heart. To dream that your lover kisses you with affection, shows that lover to be true. For married persons to dream of kissing each other, portends that they will meet with an unfaithful companion.

**Kite.**—Flying high, portends elevation in your station in life.

**Knives.**—A dream which shows that people who hate you are trying to bring you to ruin.

**Ladder.**—To be climbing a ladder is a sign that some special piece of luck will reach you. To be feeling dizzy, while climbing one, portends difficulties.

**Lamps.**—If carrying a bright lamp, it foretells that in your

particular ambition you will succeed. If with a dim, flickering light, it denotes sickness ; if the light goes out, it portends failure of your plans and hopes.

**Lark.**—It is very lucky to dream that you hear the singing of a lark. It denotes good health and prosperity.

**Laughing.**—To dream that you are laughing immoderately, denotes vexation and disappointment.

**Lightning.**—Augurs success in business and advancement to honour and independence. If the lightning be attended with rain, hail, and thunder, the dream is a bad omen.

**Linen.**—A dream about linen means an inheritance is about to come your way.

**Lion.**—To kill a lion is a sign of success and good fortune : to hear one roar means that jealous people will do you great wrongs.

**Lizards.**—A sure sign of treachery.

**Luggage.**—To be travelling with luggage which hampers your movements means that you must beware of dangers.

**Mackerel.**—A sign that evil tidings will overtake you.

**Marriage.**—It is unfortunate to dream you are married when you are not. Some evil will beset you.

**Mice.**—To dream of them means unsuccessful undertakings. Beware of your friends.

**Money.**—To dream of money is bad.

**Mountains.**—To dream of mountains in any form is good. It tells of increased wealth and love.

**Mud.**—An omen of good fortune.

**Mule.**—This creature tells of a coming lawsuit.

**Music.**—To hear music, there are pleasures in store.

**Necklace.**—Means quarrels and jealousy.

**Needles.**—You will be disappointed in love, if you are single.

**Nest.**—(Birds) Foretells marriage and domestic happiness.

**Nightingale.**—To hear one, means a happy marriage will affect your fortunes.

**Nose bleeding.**—To dream that you are bleeding at the nose, denotes that you will have sickness. To persons in business it denotes bad trade and heavy losses.

**Nosegay.**—Denotes friendship, and reciprocity in love.

**Nun.**—For a young female to dream that she has become a nun, prognosticates disappointment in love, and much sorrow.

**Oak.**—Generally foretells prosperity and long life.

**Oats.**—In almost every case, a dream of oats means added prosperity.

**Old Man.**—Good fortune awaits the dreamer.

**Old Woman.**—Scandal is likely to do you harm.

**Onions.**—To be peeling them means family troubles ; to be eating them, unexpected good fortune.

**Orange Blossom.**—Suggests a near marriage.

**Owl.**—To see or hear one tells that you must take care of your secrets.

**Painting.**—To be painting anything means domestic afflictions.

**Parrot.**—Dangerous neighbours will add to your troubles.

**Pastry.**—Sickness and pain.

**Peacock.**—Doubtful position in life ; (spreading its tail) vanity and pride.

**Pearls.**—Sorrow ; (to thread) grief and distress.

**Pheasant.**—Good fortune ; (to carry one) honour awaits you.

**Pig.**—Good fortune coming.

**Pigeon.**—Content and success will visit you.

**Pins.**—Squabbles are sure to arise.

**Play.**—(Seeing one) happiness and good fortune ; (to take part) lack of success.

**Policeman.**—Family troubles which will soon be settled.

**Postman.**—News of friends.

**Precipice.**—Dangers ; (to fall) beware of a false friend.

**Priest.**—Settlement of quarrels.

**Procession.**—Steadfast affection.

**Quarrel.**—Reunited friends.

**Rabbit.**—(Warren) costly enjoyments ; (to see rabbits) increase of family.

**Rain.**—A legacy or present.

**Rainbow.**—Estrangement.

**Rats.**—Enemies ; (white) triumph over enemies.

**Raven.**—A bad omen ; (flying) news of a death ; (croaking) sadness.

**Reptiles.**—A subtle enemy is likely to cause you pain.

**Ribbons.**—Pleasure and gaiety and foolish expenditure.

**Ring.**—Approaching wedding.

**River.**—(To fall in) envious enemies ; (to jump in) business disturbances and family troubles.

**Rock.**—Annoyance ; (to surmount) overcoming dangers.

**Room.**—(Strange) you will accomplish your designs.

**Roses.**—Always good ; (full blown) good fortune and happiness ; (faded) success with a spice of danger.

**Sailor.**—News from abroad.

**Salmon.**—Deception ; (to eat) family troubles.

**Salt.**—Good fortune and wisdom.

**Sheep.**—To see sheep feeding is a portent of great prosperity.

To see them scattered, denotes that you will meet with persecution. To see sheep-shearing indicates riches by marrying.

**Ship, or Ships.**—That you have a ship of your own sailing with merchandise, foretells riches. That you have taken a berth in a ship, denotes that you will emigrate. That you are in a ship, and it becomes leaky, is a sign that your voyage will not be successful. If a woman enceinte dreams about ships, it portends that her offspring will be a male, who will be engaged in a seafaring life.

**Shipwreck.**—Betokens misfortunes. To a lover, great disappointment in love.

**Singing.**—Foretells cause for lamentation.

**Snow.**—To see the ground covered with snow is a sign of prosperity. If in a snow-storm, you will have difficulties, but will overcome them.

**Soldiers.**—To dream that you are a soldier, foretells that you will abandon your present employment. To the tradesman it prognosticates heavy losses. To see soldiers fighting, denotes that you will be concerned in serious contentions.

**Sun.**—To dream of seeing the sun foretells success in obtaining wealth, and success in love. To see it rise, denotes good news ; to see it set, disagreeable news and losses. To see the sun overcast is a sign of trouble and great changes.

**Sweetheart.**—If you dream that your absent sweetheart is beautiful or attractive, it is a sign of constancy. If you dream that he or she is pale and sickly, it is a sign of inconstancy.

**Swimming.**—Swimming with your head above water, denotes great success in your under-

takings ; with your head under water, you will experience troubles.

**Teeth.**—To dream that your teeth are very loose, portends personal sickness ; to dream that one of them comes out, denotes the loss of a friend or relative ; to dream that they all fall out, is a sign of your own death. To dream that you have the toothache denotes much social pleasure. To dream that you cut a new tooth, denotes change of residence ; and to the married, an increase of family.

**Tempest.**—This dream indicates many troubles and losses, but you will surmount them.

**Thieves.**—To dream of thieves, is a bad dream ; it denotes loss in all cases.

**Thorns.**—To dream of thorns, portends grief, care, and difficulties.

**Trumpet.**—(To hear) sorrow and loss ; (to blow) your fortune will improve.

**Tunnel.**—Trouble in store, but it will soon pass.

**Turkey.**—Stupidity and intemperance.

**Turnips.**—Disappointment and vexation.

**Turtle-Doves.**—Affection to be bestowed.

**Unfortunate.**—(Being so) care will bring success.

**Unknown person.**—Sudden return of a long-lost one.

**Valley.**—Sickness of a temporary nature.

**Veal.**—Certain good fortune.

**Vegetables.**—Unrewarded labour ; (to gather) quarrels ; (to eat) loss in business.

**Veil.**—News of a wedding ; (black) separation.

**Velvet.**—Gain and good fortune.

**Vinegar.**—Useless toil.

**Violets.**—Success in enterprise ; (out of season) newly awakened affection.

**Vulture.**—Dangerous enemies ; (to kill) conquest of misfortune ; (to see one devouring its prey) your troubles will cease and fortune smile upon you.

**Wading.**—(Muddy water) misfortune ; (clear water) a good omen—fortune will smile on you.

**Walls.**—Dangerous enterprises and lack of success ; (easy descent from) success in business.

**Wasps.**—Dangerous enemies.

**Watch.**—A journey by land.

**Water.**—(Drinking) a bad omen ; (to fall into) reconciliation ; (bathing) misfortune and disappointments.

**Waves.**—You must be prepared to fight for fortune.

**Weasel.**—Beware of those who would appear to befriend you without reason.

**Weeding.**—Happiness and good fortune will be yours.

**Well.**—(To draw water) success and profit ; (to fall in) danger that can scarcely be avoided.

**Wheat.**—Riches will be yours.

**Wolf.**—Enmity ; (to kill) success ; (to pursue) dangers overcome ; (pursued by) dangers.

**Woodcutter.**—Your efforts will not result in much profit.

**Workhouse.**—A big legacy to come soon.

**Workshop.**—A sign of good fortune.

**Worms.**—Danger of infectious diseases.

**Writing.**—You will receive good news from an unexpected quarter.

**Zebra.**—Disagreement with friends.

# SOME POPULAR SUPERSTITIONS

## Don't

Walk under a ladder.

Wear opals, if they are not your month stone.

Light three cigarettes with the same match.

Begin a piece of important work on a Friday.

Cut your finger nails on a Sunday.

Allow peacocks' feathers to be brought into your house.

Spill salt and fail to throw a pinch over your shoulder.

Get out of bed on the wrong side.

Look at a new moon through glass.

Drop a glove and pick it up yourself.

Open an umbrella indoors.

Hang up a horseshoe with the horns pointing down.

Leave Christmas decorations hanging after Twelfth Night.

Accept a knife, a pair of scissors, or anything that cuts as a gift from a friend.

Sit down to a table so that the company numbers thirteen.

Take may-blossom into a room.

Pass anyone on the stairs of a private house.

# ANCIENT WEATHER LORE.

A red evening portends fine weather; but if it spread too far upward from the horizon in the evening, and especially morning, it foretells wind or rain, or both.

Against much rain, the clouds grow bigger, and increase very fast, especially before thunder.

A haziness in the air, which fades the sun's light, and makes the orb appear whitish, or ill-defined—or at night, if the moon and stars grow dim, and a ring encircles the former, rain will follow.

When the clouds are formed like fleeces, but dense in the middle and bright toward the edges, with the sky bright, they are signs of a frost, with hail, snow, or rain.

If clouds form high in air, in thin white trains, like locks of wool, they portend wind, and probably rain.

When a general cloudiness covers the sky, and small black fragments of clouds fly underneath, they are a sure sign of rain, and probably it will be lasting.

If the sun's rays appear like Moses's horns—if white at setting, or shorn of his rays, or goes down into a bank of clouds in the horizon, bad weather is to be expected.

If the moon look pale and dim, we expect rain; if red, wind; and if of her natural colour, with a clear sky, fair weather.

If the moon is rainy throughout, it will be clear at the change, and perhaps the rain return a few days after. If fair throughout, and rain at the change, the fair weather will probably return on the fourth or fifth day.

When the new moon is first seen lying flat on its back, it foretells a drought: if it is partially inclined, sufficiently so that a pail of water might be hung on the lower horn and not spill, it denotes fair weather; if it appears to stand nearly upright, it indicates rain, and is called a wet moon.

If a snow-storm begins at a time when the moon is young, the rising of the moon will clear the snow away.

If the dew lies plentifully on the grass after a fair day, it is the sign of another. If not, and there is no wind, rain must follow.

If there be showery weather, with sunshine, and increase of heat in the spring, a thunder-storm may be expected every day, or at least every other day.

If the wind blow between north and east, or east, with clouds, for some days, and if clouds be then seen driving from the south high up, rain will follow plentifully, sometimes forty-eight hours afterward. If, after or during the rain, the wind goes to the south or south-west; better weather.

If there be a continuance of rain from the south, it will be scarcely ever succeeded by settled weather before the wind changes, either to the west or some point of the north.

If rain fall during an east wind, it may be expected to last twenty-four hours.

If the smoke from chimneys blow down; or if soot take fire more readily than usual, or fall down the chimney into the grate; *expect rain.*

If ditches and drains smell stronger than usual, *expect rain*; as also if tobacco smoke seems denser and more powerful.

If the marigold continue shut after seven in the evening; *rain.*

If the convolvulus and chickweed close, there will be rain.

If swine be restless, and grunt loudly: if they squeak and jerk up their heads, there will be much wind; whence the proverb—"Pigs can see the wind."

If moles cast up hills; *rain*: if through openings in the frozen turf, or through a thin covering of snow, a change to open weather may be expected.

If horses stretch out their necks, and sniff the air, and assemble in the corner of a field, with their heads to leeward: *rain.*

If the fire burn unusually fierce and bright, in winter, there will be frost and clear weather; if the fire burn dull, expect damp and rain.

It seldom freezes with a west wind, not much with a north; most with a north-east, south-east, and sometimes south wind.

St...  ...mber, January, and February... ...lly one or two storms. If it bl... ...toward evening; but if it conti... ...pected to continue. The verna... ...g...s are stronger than the autumnal.

If there be long points, tails, or feathers hanging from thunder or rain clouds, five, six, or more degrees above the horizon, with little wind, in summer, thunder may be expected, but the storm will be generally of short duration.

If there be a light blue sky, with thin, light, flying clouds, whilst the wind goes to the south without much increase in force: or a dirty-blue sky, where no clouds are to be seen; storm.

If the sun be seen double, or more times reflected in the clouds, expect a heavy storm.

If the sun set with a very red sky in the east, expect stormy wind.

If two or three rings be seen round the moon, which are spotted and spread out, expect a storm of long continuance.

If there be a change from continued stormy or wet to clear and dry weather, at the time of new or full moon, or a short time before or after, and so remain until the second day of the new or full moon, it is likely to remain fine till the following quarter; and if it change not then, or only for a very short time, it usually lasts until the following new or full moon; and if it does not change then, or only for a very short time, it is likely to continue fine and dry for four or five weeks.

If the wind be north, north-west, or east, then veer to the north-east, remain there two or three days without rain, and then veer to the south without rain; and if thence it change quickly, though perhaps with a little rain, to the north-east, and remain there—such fine weather will last occasionally for two months.

Spiders generally alter their webs once in 24 hours; if they do this between six and seven in the evening, there will be a fine night; if they alter the web in the morning, a fine day; if they work during rain, expect fine weather; and the more active and busy the spider is, the finer will be the weather.